Better Decisions
Better Thinking
Better Outcomes

HOW TO GO FROM MIND FULL TO
MINDFUL LEADERSHIP

Steven Howard

Caliente Press

Better Decisions
Better Thinking
Better Outcomes
How To Go From Mind Full To Mindful Leadership

Published by:
Caliente Press
1775 E Palm Canyon Drive, Suite 110-198
Palm Springs, CA 92264
www.CalientePress.com
Email: steven@CalientePress.com

Cover Design: Kenneth Ryan Monteclaro

ENDORSEMENTS AND PRAISE

The world is becoming more complicated, and making good decisions is both more important and increasingly difficult. This book helps you understand what's happening to our brains, and what we can do about it.

Wayne Turmel
Co-Author
The Long-Distance Leader:
Rules for Remarkable Remote Leadership

Better Decisions. Better Thinking. Better Outcomes. How to go from Mind Full to Mindful Leadership. by Steven Howard is an engaging read full of great advice for busy leaders who want to be more effective and to lead with both heart and mind.

Supported by research, each chapter unpacks concrete strategies for the busy professional to become more mindful about their approach to leadership in any organization. This is a book I will definitely recommend to colleagues who are succumbing to the expected stresses and challenges of leadership. This book will help you be your best self!

Susan Rice, Head of School
Palm Valley School

Steven mentions LEADERSHIP as both a Science and an Art. After reading this book I would also add Craft. Steven not only gives us a motivational framework in which to apply Leadership but additionally provides practical steps and exercises to deepen our pursuit towards leadership excellence. Even while reading, his enthusiasm and style moved me to begin my own practice. As you read, you will want to have pen and paper at the ready for frequent notes and tips.

John Petraborg
Global Leadership Development Facilitator

Steven Howard's new book *Better Decisions. Better Thinking. Better Outcomes.* provides the variables that cause "mind full" leaders to make bad decisions. Unconscious biases caught my attention as they negatively impact gender-related decisions daily.

Readers are provided with excellent mindfulness techniques that will enable them to move from "mind full" to "mindful" leadership and deliver better outcomes for their organizations.

Lynn Schmidt, PhD
Author, Shift Into Thrive:
Six Strategies for Women to Unlock the Power of Resiliency

Seasoned judgment is essential to great leadership, because leaders are called to make bold, thoughtful, and wise decisions. Sweeping in scope and rich in value, this book will help your leadership gain focus, stamina, and enjoyment. As the title suggests, when you make better decisions, have better thinking, and get better outcomes, you become a better leader.

Bill Treasurer
bestselling author of Leaders Open Doors

Mindfulness — it is not something that we really think about. As a business leader, it is about making that optimum decision at a given point of time. Unfortunately, between juggling life, work, stress and constant deadlines, we forget to nourish the one muscle that is making all these decisions – our brain. This book reminds us the importance. *Better Decisions. Better Thinking. Better Outcomes.* is packed full of tips, steps and techniques on how to boost your brain power that leads to better decision-making. Not just better decision-making, but also becoming a better leader!

Alex Chan
CEO, Babbobox
Singapore

As leaders, we all make less-than-optimal decisions at times that produce poor or inadequate results. Steven Howard's book explains why this happens and how to make better decisions and create more desirable outcomes for ourselves, our colleagues, and our organizations.

William Carlson
President
Tucker/Hall Public Relations and Communications Consulting

Better Decisions. Better Thinking. Better Outcomes focuses on one of the most challenging aspects of modern-day leadership — how to be a positive force in the midst of VUCA. Steven has moved the discussion away from the symptoms of poor decision making to an understanding of its root causes and how to deal with them. Chapter after Chapter offer practical steps for personal development and insights in how to keep mind and body in harmony.

William F. Molloy
Leadership Development Coach and Facilitator
FORTUNE 500 companies

Contents

Dedication

*This book is dedicated to my three children:
Ryan, Patrick and Diani*

*With the hopes that its contents
will spur better decisions, better thinking, and
better outcomes in your own lives.*

The mind is like water.

When it is turbulent, blocked or agitated
it is difficult to see clearly.

When it is calmed, freed and unencumbered,
everything becomes clearer.

Introduction

There are two major health trends happening in the United States — and in fact around many parts of the world — that should be highly concerning to both leaders and societies.

The first is the aging and rapidly increasing obesity in the Baby Boomer generation. This is the generation of retirees, almost retirees, and the eldest portion of today's workforce. Why is this a concern? Because this generation is entering a period when increasing dementia will be seen, both as a result of fairly inactive retirement living and the negative impact on brain and cardiovascular health resulting from excessive weight and poor dietary habits.

Partially for these reasons, current estimates predict that some 76 million people around the world, including over 10 million in the United States, will be struggling with dementia a decade from now. This will be an increase of over 60% from today's levels. By 2030, treating Alzheimer's disease, other forms of dementia, and stroke will be a $1 trillion industry.

Unlike physical health, people rarely consider or think about what they could or should be doing for the health of their brains. This is sad because Alzheimer's related brain changes start as early as our 30s and 40s. This is why it is not just Baby Boomers who are at risk. Frightfully, according to estimates by the American Heart Association and the American Stroke Association, 60% of Americans will develop a brain disease in their lifetime.

Fortunately, there is an increasing amount of scientific research suggesting we can improve the health of our brains no matter what age we are. The best time to start a brain improvement plan? Now. The sooner you start the sooner you can make your brain stronger and protect it for the long term.

The other troubling trend is produced by Generation X (those born in the years 1965 through 1979) and Millennials (those born in the years 1980 through 2000) to habitually engage in multitasking and to live lives that are tethered to mobile devices and constantly susceptible to electronic notifications. All of these beeps, buzzes, and electronic chimes are activating unconscious stress signals in their bodies. This long-term accumulation of such constant stress is wearing down their brains, with long-term consequences for brain health and future hypertension readings.

No wonder Generation X (the bulk of day's workforce, frontline leaders, and senior leaders) has been identified by the American Psychological Association as the most stressed generation in the United States.

In addition, their multitasking habits are creating brains that are losing the ability to concentrate and focus. Unfortunately, losing these abilities is a precursor to Alzheimer's disease and other forms of dementia. The research is clear: multitasking diminishes productivity, elevates brain fatigue, and increases stress. Yet this has become the main operational mode for many.

These are alarming trends — for companies, organizations, and societies.

Fortunately, they are also reversible trends. But only if the leaders in companies, organizations, governments, and societies take the proper steps — first with themselves and then with their peers, employees, spouses, children, neighbors, and communities.

Another worrying trend — one with growing daily impact — is the increase in the number of Baby Boomers who are having to be caregivers to elderly parents and spouses crippled by dementia. As one who helped his own father cope with short-term memory loss and a gradual decline in cognitive abilities for the last four-plus years of his life, I can attest that this is a difficult task for which most of us have not been trained.

As lifespans lengthen, adult children in their 60s and 70s are increasingly caring for frail, older parents. An analysis from the Center for Retirement Research at Boston College found that 10% of adults ages 60 to 69 whose parents are alive serve as parental caregivers, as do 12% of adults age 70 and older.

The financial and emotional difficulties of these situations will undoubtedly increase for years to come. If you do not want to be a burden to your own children, you must start making some critical lifestyle changes now. After all, brain health is a lifetime pursuit, not something to be pushed off until your elderly years.

My research into Alzheimer's disease began when I started to assist my father. After his passing my research intensified, mostly for selfish reasons (I certainly do not wish to live my final years in cognitive decline). As I conducted my research, I was thrilled to learn of new neuroscientific studies showing that neuroplasticity — the ability to grow neuronal connectivity across the brain — can continue well into our 70s. I was one of those who believed our brains stopped growing new cells in our mid-twenties.

Likewise, I was astonished to read report after report showing direct links between mindfulness and meditation with the thickening of brain regions, increases in cognitive capabilities, and reductions in the areas of the brain that trigger stress hormones and emotional outbursts.

9

And most important, I was ecstatic to read about new scientific research showing that mindfulness, meditation, and better dietary habits could slow and even postpone the debilitating effects of dementia and Alzheimer's disease.

Additionally, as I started to learn how stress and poor dietary habits lead to bad decisions, poor thinking, and undesirable outcomes, I began to see brain health as not just a personal health issue, but also a professional, work-related issue not being addressed by companies or organizations.

When I started to link recent scientific research into brain health with my own work in leadership development, it became painfully obvious that leaders are not fully aware of how stress triggers poor decisions. More important, leaders have not been trained in how to become cognizant of when stress is triggering them toward poor decision making. It was also obvious that very few leaders are aware of the many benefits that mindfulness practices will bring to their decision-making processes and thinking capabilities.

Everyone knows about the benefits of aerobic exercise and proper nutrition on cardiovascular and overall health. Yet so few people are aware of how exercise, nutrition, and mindfulness can positively impact short-term and long-term brain health.

And while such benefits may be intuitively clear, they are not enough to motivate action and spur behavioral change. At least not with the dozens of leaders I spoke with. The common responses I got were "sounds great" and "most interesting." Unfortunately, factual information on brain health alone was not going to spark action.

However, once I started illustrating how reducing stress and increasing brain health would lead to better decisions, improved thinking and analytical capabilities, and more desirable outcomes, I had their full attention.

And that is what I hope to do with you, dear reader. Grab your full attention. Show you the facts about how exercise and diet impact your brain. Share with you some of the latest neuroscientific research on how mindfulness and meditation practices actually help you grow new brain neurons and increase cellular connectivity across your brain.

Perhaps most important, I also want to help you find ways to prevent emotions from hijacking your rational, cognitive resources, thus enabling you to make better decisions, think more rationally, and reduce emotional meltdowns and outbursts.

And that is the reason for the order of decisions, thinking, and outcomes in this book's title. The more linear approach would have been to call this book *Better Thinking. Better Decisions. Better Outcomes.* After all, thinking leads to decisions and these in turn lead to outcomes.

But I purposely changed this order to *Better Decisions. Better Thinking. Better Outcomes.* This is because the first decision people need to make is to become mindful, in order to facilitate a better thinking process. The current linear mode of thinking >> decisions >> outcomes is being impacted by stress, overtaxed brains, information overload, etc. So the first step to better thinking — and better outcomes — is to make the decision not to get emotionally hijacked by your overloaded brain, in order to move into a rational thinking mode.

There is also a larger goal inherent in this book. We live in a highly divisive, argumentative, agitated, and spring-loaded world. Workplace stress is at an all-time high, as is workplace violence and fear. Incidents of rage, verbal abuse, and physical confrontations are increasing at all levels of society, from elementary schools through to boardrooms and community associations and right on through to our national political discourse.

I believe stress and our overloaded brains are two of the underlying causes creating so much conflict, tension, and drama at the human interaction level, both in the workplace and in non-work related interactions. As a result, the tendency is to react to situations, events, and people abruptly and emotionally. As a society, and as human beings, we need to create a new predisposition to pause and then respond instead of react. Remember, our emergency personnel are called First Responders, not First Reactors. If they reacted, instead of responding, in emergency situations the results would be dreadful.

It is not that we have forgotten how to be kind, humane, and just. It simply seems that such attributes are too often considered weaknesses, or easily subdued in favor of clashing, confrontation, rudeness, and a non-collaborative approach to interpersonal interactions.

What kind of world are we creating and leaving for our children and grandchildren?

It is time that individually and collectively we start working harder to change the divisive mindsets, aggressive attitudes, and bad behaviors that are percolating through our communities, schools, and workplaces. We all need to do a better job of responding — rationally, empathetically, and compassionately — to situations, events, and people. Doing so produces better outcomes and fewer regrets, in both our professional and personal lives.

So I hope this book stirs new habits in helping you to cognitively respond, instead of emotionally react, to situations and other people. I hope it arouses a desire to not only find greater peace and solitude in your life, but to also spread these messages and benefits to others. And I hope it generates an eagerness in you to bring the concepts and ideas of this book formally into your own organization, business unit, or work team, either through the workshops my associates and I deliver or through your own enthusiastic practices and behaviors.

Together we can make your organizations less stressful, more engaging, more productive, and happier places to work. Now, wouldn't that be a wonderful outcome for you and your fellow colleagues and team members?

Lastly, there is a third goal for this book and our associated programs on moving from a *mind full* to a mindful leader and person. And that is to cascade the information in this book wide and far so we can collectively reduce those troubling and worrying statistics on Alzheimer's disease and dementia shown above.

By helping ourselves, and one another, take the proper steps to enhance brain health, we can reduce the financial costs to society — and the brutal emotional costs to families — of dementia and Alzheimer's disease.

There is no excuse for allowing a 60% increase in the number of people suffering from dementia. This is preventable, but the right actions need to be taken now — by you, your family members, your work colleagues, and everyone else. I am counting on you to help spread this message. And so are your loved ones, family members, co-workers, and friends.

If you would like to be part of our global information dissemination team, please contact me. We are creating Certified Trainer Programs and Mindful Leaders MasterMind groups to provide on-going support, materials, and tools for those who truly want to apply the information and techniques in this book within their organizations and communities.

In the meantime, please enjoy this book and reflect on the many lessons it has to offer. The techniques described will help you make better decisions and improve your thinking prowess. They will also result in you becoming a less stressed and far healthier person.

And that, I am sure you would agree, are definitely four better outcomes that will definitely benefit you immediately, and for years to come.

Best wishes for continued success.

Steven Howard
October 2018

CHAPTER 1

Leadership and Mindfulness

L eadership, as I define it, is the art of achieving progress through the involvement and actions of others. This makes leadership both an art and a science, though I daresay it is more art than science.

Mindfulness, as defined by Jon Kabat-Zinn means "paying attention in a particular way, on purpose, in the present moment, and nonjudgmentally." Mindfulness is a mental state achieved by focusing awareness on the present moment, while calmly acknowledging and accepting one's feelings, thoughts, and bodily sensations.

So, what does one have to do with the other? Aren't leaders constantly aware of the present situations and challenges facing them?

Unfortunately, the honest answer is no. Some will be at times, but the large majority are not fully present and mindfully aware of present situations and circumstance, nor of the thoughts and feelings of those around them. This is especially true for the mid-level leaders in organizations who constantly feel pressures from both below and above to execute, lead, juggle, and make decisions with insufficient information and inadequate time.

One of the main reasons leaders are not fully present and aware of situations is the tremendous stress they are under caused by deadlines, decisions made by others, internal politics, career concerns, the pressures associated with personal financial stability, and the need for continuing their personal income flows.

These daily pressures and stresses accumulate and result in poor or less-than-optimal decision making by leaders at all levels of all organizations.

And that is where mindfulness comes in. As both a barrier and an antidote to the many disrupting stresses and pressures leaders face and confront. It is a prescriptive remedy, backed by recent rigorous scientific research, that the majority of leaders are neither aware of nor utilize. While mindfulness practices, and the resultant benefits for decision making, thinking, and outcomes, have gotten a foothold within many Silicon Valley organizations, it has yet to become a mainstream skill for leaders. This needs to change.

But before I share with you some of the scientific results on the positive impact of mindfulness on leadership and decision making, let me clear the air on several common misconceptions about mindfulness and its application for leaders. Mindfulness does not mandate that you take up yoga, burn incense, go on ten-day silent retreats, or meditate several times a day. While those are all elements of various mindfulness practices, none are required to increase your own mindfulness levels.

There are many myths and misconceptions about mindfulness, so to clear any confusion let's be clear:

1. Mindfulness is more than just learning to meditate. In fact, meditation is not required to become more mindful and present.

2. The purpose of mindfulness is to slow down and observe thoughts without judgment, not to have zero thoughts.

3. Mindfulness is not about taking time out to relax, rest, and tune-out the world. Instead, mindfulness helps you become more attuned and aware of the world around you.

4. The ultimate goal is not to become mindful all the time, but rather to bring mindfulness into your life on a regular basis to reduce stress, control emotions, improve cognitive thinking, and make better decisions.

And in terms of applying mindfulness to leadership, there is also no need for your leadership team to gather together in circles singing *Kumbaya*. Rather, as this book will show, mindfulness is a management technique that enables leaders to make higher quality decisions, enhance cognitive thinking skills, improve employee engagement, increase productivity, and produce more desirable results, while simultaneously improving their own health and reducing their risks for high blood pressure, cardiac incidents, and Alzheimer's disease.

Mindfulness

Mindfulness has its roots in Buddhism. However, Buddhism is no more a religion than yoga. You can improve your body and your mental state through yoga without becoming a Hindu. Likewise, you can improve your brain and mental state through mindful meditation without becoming a Buddhist. Think of mindful meditation as a secular methodology for improving your mental muscles and cognitive acuity.

In recent years, mindfulness has been the subject of extensive research, with many studies confirming that the practice provides significant physical and mental health benefits, particularly for those exposed to continued elevated levels of stress and workplace pressure (i.e. the state in which most leaders operate a great deal of the time).

Many of the exact mechanisms of how mindfulness positively improves physical and mental health remain unknown. However, several scientists and scientific studies hypothesize that the health benefits of mindfulness are caused by four interrelated factors: attention regulation, body awareness, purposefully altering self-perception, and emotion regulation. Each of these areas directly impacts leadership behavior and actions.

Here's an overview of these four key factors:

> Attention regulation is the ability to maintain almost complete awareness on an object or thought during meditation, such as one's breathing pattern, a mantra, or a self-selected thought. Proficiency in this area comes from gently and repeatedly bringing one's own attention back to the object of meditation when distracted. Training in such situational attention assists in developing positive emotions and increasing the ability to focus and concentrate during non-meditative moments.

> Body awareness is simply increasing one's ability to monitor the many sensations and signals of the body. This helps to foster increased emotional awareness and regulation. It also prompts increased empathetic responses to the feelings and emotions of others without feeling overwhelmed.

Many meditative practitioners employ a concept known as "body scan" during meditation sessions to enhance body awareness capabilities.

Altering self-perception is the ability to see one's self as impermanent and changing. This comes from the Buddhist belief that believing the self to be permanent and unchanging is the core cause of psychological stress. Being adaptable is a core component of dealing with change. It is also an essential mindset to have, since life is a series of perpetual change.

Emotion regulation is the ability to check, adjust, and control one's emotional responses through an assortment of techniques and strategies. Emotions and their related bodily responses are to be accepted, which facilitates emotional wellbeing and the rising and passing of emotions. In other words, you are entitled to your own emotions and feelings, and trying to bottle these up, hide them, or deny them causes problems. It is best to accept one's emotions, knowing that they are impermanent and will pass in time. At the same time, regulating how emotions are expressed prevents regrettable actions and words and leads to better thinking and outcomes.

While you definitely should not believe everything you read or hear about mindfulness (there are many over-jealous proponents out there spreading unsubstantiated claims), there is no doubt that mindfulness and meditation practices provide significant payoffs to those who inculcate these methods into their daily habits. Mindfulness is not a panacea for everything a leader faces, but it does help improve many aspects of life and health.

And it costs nothing, except for a little dedicated time and self-monitoring.

However, what makes mindfulness especially appealing is that a combination of a few quiet reflective moments, some deep breaths, and a greater awareness (and appreciation) of the present moment can (and will) create a sense of internal calmness that no pharmaceutically produced pill can match.

In fact, according to an article in *Harvard Business Review*, research also shows that the more hours of meditation you put in over your lifetime, the better your results will be. Like any skill, the more practice and time spent on it, the greater will be your mindfulness proficiency and expertise.

One way to develop a mindfulness habit is to think of mindfulness as a way to enhance various aspects of your mental fitness, just as regular jogging or gym workouts build your physical fitness.

Mindfulness is a Leadership Skill

While mindfulness may sound like some kind of a new fad, due to the increased media coverage on the subject, it is actually a leadership skill that goes back several decades. A recent article in *Harvard Business Review* notes that Pierre Wack, head of Group Planning at Royal Dutch Shell in the 1970s and the famed creator of scenario planning, studied meditation extensively with teachers in Asia over forty years ago. Planning well, according to Wack, required "training the mind."

Quieting the mind, the essence of mindfulness, allows us to be cognitively receptive to new, and especially unexpected, sources of information. As Jim Butcher wrote in *Harvard Business Review* (May 2018), "mindfulness can help leaders to see past the storylines and narratives that unconsciously guide their traditional thinking. This can help individuals and firms break free from the tyranny of unexamined assumptions."

I agree with Butcher's assertion that mindfulness is more than a mental fitness tool. As he says, "it's an asset for leaders seeking to perceive — and re-perceive — the world and make better strategic choices."

Perhaps this is why meditation — a core conduit (but not a prerequisite) to mindfulness — is practiced by so many corporate leaders, including Ray Dalio, founder of Bridgewater Associates; Russell Simmons, Chair and CEO of Rush Communications; Jeff Weiner, CEO at LinkedIn; Marc Benioff, founder of SalesForce; and Bill Ford, executive chairman of Ford Motor Company.

Workplace implementation is not limited to just the C-suites, either. Aetna has fully incorporated mindfulness into its corporate culture, including creating the position of a Chief Mindfulness Officer. According to an article in *Healthy Workplace*, participants in Aetna's corporate-wide mindfulness program are "regaining 62 minutes per week of productivity." This approximates to roughly $3000 per person per annum in productivity gains for the insurance giant.

Other companies employing various types of mindfulness and meditation programs for employees include Google, Goldman Sachs, General Mills, Intel, Nike, and Apple. In fact, a study conducted jointly by Fidelity Investments and the National Business Group on Health revealed that approximately 20% of the companies surveyed offer mindfulness training to employees, with another 21% planning to do so in the near future. It has been estimated that mindfulness training is already a $1B-plus industry in the U.S. and growing exponentially at a rapid pace.

As a leader, mindfulness is the habit of pausing and checking in with yourself during times of stress or when things are getting chaotic and out of control. By pausing, and using the mindfulness techniques described in chapter 14, leaders can take their brains off autopilot mode and truly engage with the here and now. It is effectively a conscious mindset switch, which makes it a skill you can learn, practice, and master.

Mindfulness can also help you detect negative emotions as they arise, and learn ways to keep these from escalating into emotional outbursts or meltdowns. By being more mindful of your body, you can detect tension, anxiety, doubt, and other feelings as they start to occur, rather than after you have been emotionally hijacked. Mindfulness taps into the signals your body sends you, such as faster heartbeats, tensing of muscles, queasiness in the gut, and shallow breathing, all of which are physical signals related to negative emotions and feelings.

The Science Behind Mindfulness

Entire books are being written on the numerous scientific studies validating the benefits of mindfulness. If you are interested in in-depth exposure to these studies, I highly recommend:

> *Train Your Mind, Change Your Brain: How a New Science Reveals Our Extraordinary Potential to Transform Ourselves* by Sharon Begley

> *The Leading Brain: Power Science-Based Strategies for Achieving Peak Performance* by Friederike Fabritius and Hans W. Hagemann

> *Super Brain: Unleashing the Explosive Power of Your Mind to Maximize Health, Happiness, and Spiritual Well-Being* by Deepak Chopra and Rudolph E. Tanzi

Make Your Brain Smarter: Increase Your Brain's Creativity, Energy, and Focus by Sandra Bond Chapman

Hard scientific research, along with personal reporting of self-perceived benefits, has overwhelmingly shown that mindfulness is beneficial both cognitively and emotionally. Proving the impact of mindfulness on brain structure or functionality was impossible until only a few years ago. Today, however, with tools such as magnetic resonance imaging (MRI) machines, scientists have started to reveal how mindfulness alters both brain architecture and functionality.

Richard Davidson, a psychologist at the University of Wisconsin Madison, has authored over 30 studies on mindfulness and its effect on how the brain works. "Over the past 10 or 12 years," notes Davidson, "there has been a vibrant interest in sectors of the neuroscientific community in studying the impact of meditation. We can look at brain structure and function and study people repeatedly over time to see how practicing mindfulness and meditation impact the brain and change behavior and experiences."

In the past decade, numerous scientific studies have shown that practicing mindfulness techniques can change a person's brain chemistry and the synaptic links impacting memory, recall, and emotional regulation.

In one of the more recent studies, Harvard neuroscientists employed brain-imaging techniques to examine the neurobiological effects arising from mindfulness training. The study compared the brain scans of two groups, one which underwent eight weeks of mindfulness-based stress reduction training and a control group that did not participate in the training program.

The study found that the participants in the mindfulness-based stress reduction program had significant changes in five major regions of their brains compared to the control group. This included a thickening in the areas of the brain responsible for memory, learning, cognition, perspective, emotional regulation, empathy, and compassion. Additionally, those participants from the mindfulness training program also showed a reduction in the areas of their brains that produce the hormones related to anxiety, stress, and fear.

This is far from the only scientific study to demonstrate the significant positive changes that mindfulness has on the brain. A 2016 study, published in *Biological Psychiatry*, revealed that people who meditated for as little as a few hours over the course of three days experienced improvements in mental functioning. Furthermore, brain scans of these participants indicated decreased inflammation compared to a control group that did not meditate. They also exhibited an improved ability to stay calm in difficult, stressful situations.

Even more remarkable, however, is that although many of the participants in the experiment did not continue to meditate on their own after the initial experiment period, the inflammation levels in their brains remained lower than the control group a full four months later. This indicates that even short periods of meditation can have a long-lasting impact on the physical characteristics of the brain.

Additionally, a research study published in *Frontiers in Psychology* showed that including just a few minutes of meditative stillness and deep breathing in one's daily routine has the ability to protect the brain from the cognitive risks associated with aging, including slowing down the rate at which the brain naturally decreases in volume and begins to shrink.

As the aforementioned Richard Davidson wrote in an article in *Scientific American*, "The discovery of meditation's benefits coincides with recent neuroscientific findings showing that the adult brain can still be deeply transformed through experience." It is becoming evidently clear that some of the best experiences for one's brain come through meditation and mindfulness practices.

Mindfulness for Leaders

Mindfulness is the polar opposite of being in a *mind full* mode.

It is a choice on how you want to live, both professionally and personally.

For leaders, mindfulness is not just about improving the ability to have greater control over your thoughts. It is also important and beneficial for greatly reducing the control your unconscious and habitual thoughts have over your actions and emotions.

You are going to have thoughts anyway. It is just a matter of whether you or your thoughts are going to be in control.

To regain control over your thoughts it is necessary to disengage the autopilot mode within which so many leaders operate. Yes, working on autopilot does seem to be highly effective and productive. However, similar to the belief that multitasking is an efficient methodology for accomplishing a lot, both methods sacrifice quality for quantity and can have a negative impact on interpersonal relationships.

Mindfulness also brings into focus two critical components of leadership success: intention and presence.

As a leader, you are a leader of people. As Rear Admiral Grace Murray Hopper said, "You manage things. You lead people." In order to be successful in leading people, you have to be well grounded in both your intentions and your presence.

For every interaction with people, great leaders pause and set their intentions. Intention is the approach and behavior you will bring into the interaction, be it support, perspective, authority, accountability, positivity, or even vulnerability. Your intention must be based on your values and your sense of what the people you lead need, at that moment, in order to be successful. By being mindful, you will not enter a meeting with only the objective of "reviewing action plans," but rather also with the intention of providing whatever is needed for your team members to be successful and thrive.

Of course, to do this you also have to be fully present. That is where mindful presence comes in. Active participation in a discussion requires giving full attention to everyone present. It means actively listening to not only what is being said, but also to what is not being said. What unspoken agendas are in play? What are you not being told because of fear or unease? How deeply do your people believe in what they are telling you?

Being fully present means not thinking about other issues and topics that may be going on in your world. It means not taking surreptitious glances at your phone or computer to see what emails or text messages have arrived or who is trying to reach you. Fully present means giving your full attention and focus to what is being said during the interaction.

This is why mindfulness is an important leadership skill, albeit one that is not being taught in many leadership development programs. Fortunately, this is changing. For the evidence is becoming overwhelming: when practiced by leaders at all levels of an organization, mindfulness results in better decisions, better thinking, and better outcomes.

And, as you will see in the next chapter, becoming more mindful throughout the workday can help prevent a whole slew of leadership derailment issues.

CHAPTER 2

Leadership Derailment

L eadership derailment often comes as a blind-sided shock to leaders. But it shouldn't. Postmortem explanations for the root causes of leaders going off the rails usually boils down to one or more commonly seen factors:

- Self-doubt and a drop in self-confidence causing poor thinking and analysis.

- Too much focus and worry about potential negative outcomes.

- Cognitive overload resulting from busy brain syndrome.

- Inability to handle distractions, resulting in poor focus.

Here is what leadership derailment feels like. One moment you are the person in charge with the undisputed voice of authority, the driver of results. And then, without warning and seemingly from out of the shadows appear little erosions and self-doubt in your leadership capabilities. At first, these go unnoticed. Then small, illuminating signs make their appearance on a gradually more frequent basis.

You start to question your decisions, and so do others (silently at first and then verbally). You become hesitant to make decisions that previously were routine. Postponing action, under the guise of waiting for more data, turns from an occasional occurrence into a habit.

You run around hurriedly getting lots of things done, but nothing strategic or of importance seems to get accomplished. Outcomes and results still show some progress but are not up to your expectations or those of your boss.

And then the big questions really hit home: are you cut out for this leadership thing? Or should you revert to the individual contributor role at which you previously excelled? Additionally, you start to wonder if your leadership role has become a title only, an empty shell unsupported by your actions, thoughts, and decisions.

Another leadership derailment illness occurs when leaders become disassociated with their team or individual direct reports. Symptoms of this kind of derailment include either isolation or heightened micromanaging, both of which create problems for professional working relationships. They also impact decision making and the outcomes produced by the team or individual team members.

In a March 2018 article in *Harvard Business Review* titled The Most Common Type of Incompetent Leader, Scott Gregory wrote, "The key determinant characteristics of bad managers are well documented and fall into three broad behavior categories: 1) moving away behaviors, 2) moving against behaviors, and 3) moving toward behaviors."

Gregory writes that "moving away behaviors" create distance from others through hyper-emotionality, diminished communications, and skepticism that erodes trust. Behaviors that overpower and manipulate people while aggrandizing the self he labels as "moving against behaviors." Lastly, the "moving toward behaviors" include being ingratiating, overly conforming, and a reluctance to take chances or stand up for one's team.

All of these behavior categories are bad habits that leaders can easily fall into. I would advocate that the key causes of these derailment habits are workload pressures, multitasking, constant interruptions throughout the typical workday, and the resultant inability to spend sufficient time and focus on the important rather than the urgent. These are also the signs of being a *mind full* leader.

Heike Bruch and Sumantra Ghoshal hit the nail on the head in their *Harvard Business Review* article Beware the Busy Manager. A major conclusion from their ten years of studying the behaviors of busy managers in nearly a dozen large companies is that, "Very few managers use their time as effectively as they could. They think they are attending to pressing matters, but they are really just spinning their wheels."

Now that is truly being derailed, especially for more senior leaders and executives. In fact, according to Bruch and Ghoshal, "Fully 90% of managers squander their time in all sorts of ineffective activities. In other words, a mere 10% of managers spend their time in a committed, purposeful, and reflective manner." Committed, purposeful, and reflective are, along with fully focused and attentive, the core essences of being a mindful leader.

These are frightening numbers. And, in my experience, they are equally true in medium-sized organizations, small businesses, and even non-profit entities. Everyone is so busy running around getting "stuff" done, and constantly interrupting each other in the guise of communication and collaboration, that leaders and managers are left without sufficient time and energy for reflection, innovative thinking, exploring out-of-the-box options, and creating purposeful action.

That, combined with a focus on quarterly results and yearly performance goals, negates the opportunity for innovative thinking and ideas that might create long-term, sustainable success for the organization and its people. Instead, in many organizations leaders only have time to tackle short-term projects and continue to run on autopilot mode until the next crisis smacks them in the organizational face.

As a result, the juggling leaders of today make rapid-fire decisions based on previous experiences or situations, even when the data, market conditions, and competitive initiatives require new solutions and ideas. Even if leaders found the time for innovative and out-of-the-box thinking, chances are their brains are too fried and exhausted to fully engage in such high-quality cognitive pursuits.

In summary, too many leaders are operating in *mind full* mode too often. This is causing poor thinking, unnecessary worries, overloaded brains, reduced cognitive functioning, drops in self-confidence, and an inability to focus and pay attention. Fortunately, all these ailments are fixable through mindfulness practices, as you will discover throughout this book. But first, let's take a deeper look at how our busy brains and the constant distractions we face impact our abilities to think clearly, make better decisions, and produce more desirable outcomes.

The Busy Brain

Our brains are amazing. They control our bodily functions. They recall past events. They provide us with lucid dreams while we sleep or nap.

But our brains are also annoying. They never shut off! They continually crave new information, data, and experiences to process. In today's world, they also cannot seem to go a dozen minutes without needing to check email, Twitter, Instagram, or Facebook. Remarkably, research studies have shown that the average person accesses their mobile phone up to 110 times a day (you can now blame your brain's persistent need for new information to process for this incessant craving).

The popular acronym FOMO stands for Fear Of Missing Out. I sincerely suggest it should really be a warning of Fear of Mind Overload. All that fear of missing out on something, even something trivial or minor like where a friend is eating lunch, is definitely causing our minds and brains to be overloaded.

Fortunately, we can change our ability to focus by changing our behavior. And it is easier than you might think. However, it does require immense dedication and fortitude.

The key is to purposefully put away anything that might distract you during periods when focus is paramount. For instance, while I have been writing this book I have set my mobile phone to airplane mode. This prevents me from being distracted by any electronic notifications, incoming phone calls, or new text messages. For the remainder of the morning, nothing is more important than writing this draft and this process prevents the urgent from also getting in the way.

After three to four hours of focused writing, I will then turn off airplane mode to check messages and email. The urgent ones will be responded to immediately at that time. The others can wait until later in the day when the draft of this chapter is completed. And tomorrow I will implement this same process again.

Since I do need to maintain regular, on-going contact with the outside world (such as my clients), despite being in what I call "writing mode," I simply batch all email, text messaging, and social media interactions into designated blocks of time when I need some respite from writing. Knowing myself well, I know that these blocks of time will take place every three to four hours, depending on how the writing is progressing.

Likewise, I have arranged for all scheduled phone conversations and conference calls to take place on Wednesday this week. Non-urgent email replies and other tasks, such as paying bills and grocery shopping, will also take place on Wednesday. By grouping all these activities into the same day, Wednesday becomes my scheduled non-writing day for the week. This also gives my brain a one-day break from focusing on the content of this book, a kind of "day at the beach" for my own busy brain.

Another way to get control over one's busy brain is through taking several short breaks during the course of the day. If you are desk-bound or corralled all day in meeting rooms, a few short walks around the office or outside provides a much-needed respite for an overloaded mind.

Even a social, non-work related phone call gives your brain something to focus on outside the information overload being experienced in the workplace.

There is also a natural chemical way to control your busy brain and increase your focus — boost your levels of serotonin.

Serotonin is an important chemical and neurotransmitter produced by the body. It plays a significant role in many bodily functions and also assists in stabilizing moods, reducing depression, increasing libido, controlling sleep, and regulating anxiety.

Importantly, serotonin also regulates delayed gratification. When serotonin levels are low, the ability to wait for gratification reduces. As a result, the ability to focus on an important task or mental challenge is lost in favor of the instant gratification that comes from short-term pleasures such as shopping, television viewing, online gaming, eating, or talking with friends or family members. Even the instant gratification of completing non-essential tasks, such as reading emails or completing an expense report, can outweigh working on an important task when serotonin levels dip too low.

Serotonin levels are quickly boosted through exercise. They can also be increased by recalling past positive life events. According to Alex Korb, a neuroscientist at UCLA and author of *The Upward Spiral*, the simple act of remembering positive events "increases serotonin production in the anterior cingulate cortex, which is a region just behind the prefrontal cortex that controls attention."

Hence taking charge of your busy brain and regaining attention and focus is straight-forward. Increase serotonin production through exercise or positive memory recall and the likelihood of increased attention span rises significantly. Now, if you could just control those annoying distractions emanating from others!

Battling Distractions

Scientific research tells us that as we age we are more easily distracted by irrelevant information, particularly when experiencing stress or powerful emotions. "Increased distractibility is a sign of cognitive aging," says Professor Mara Mather, an expert on memory at the USC Leonard Davis School of Gerontology. This is not good news for senior leaders, the majority of whom are no longer classified as young adults.

While we will discuss the impact of stress on decision making in chapter four, there can be little doubt that stress also deteriorates one's ability to focus. Here again, the mindfulness techniques in chapter 14 can be used to help regain focus and drown out environmental disturbances such as noises and sounds.

We also know from research that multitasking is detrimental to focus. It will be interesting to see if the penchant for multitasking via electronic devices by the Millennial Generation will speed up distractibility as they age. This predilection for multitasking is certainly not training their brains on the skill of focus.

Handling a multitude of low-level decisions, especially early in the day, can be distracting and cognitively consuming. For one thing, doing so reduces the full supply of cognitive resources the brain has after a good night's sleep.

Thus, it is far better to handle the most challenging mental tasks early in the day when cognitive resources are at a peak. This is why some people now try to eliminate as many low-level choices, ranging from what to wear to what to eat, in the morning. Some, like Steve Jobs and Mark Zuckerberg, even go to the extent of wearing the same outfits every day. Personally, I would not take it to that extreme, but to each their own.

However, I do counsel leaders to use the morning period for extremely mentally taxing tasks such as brainstorming, evaluating options, absorbing new information, delivering feedback, and writing strategic documents. The last thing leaders should be doing to start their day is holding a series of project status meetings or reviewing budget projections.

Speaking of which, when is the brain most rested, from a work perspective? Probably on Monday mornings after a series of non-work related weekend activities. So the greatest waste of one's rested brain power would be to engage in a weekly 9am team meeting on Monday mornings of round-the-table information sharing and routine work planning sessions. Better to use that time slot for something more meaningful, while the cognitive resource tank is full.

For this reason, I now advise leaders to never schedule weekly staff meetings on Monday mornings before 11am. After lunch is an even better time. After all, the cognitive resources of their staffs are also filled to the brim in the morning and should not be wasted or drained through mundane weekly staff meetings.

As mentioned before, multitasking is not truly a productive way to lead, nor to accomplish major tasks. While it may seem like doing lots of things at once is the height of efficiency, the constant switching between email correspondence, phone conversations, and other task activities prevents the brain from focusing and engaging in deep problem-solving cognitive processing.

Yes, the brain will get a dollop of dopamine through the self-satisfaction and rewarding feelings that come from knocking a multitude of items off the to-do list. However, this is usually a short-term hit similar to the short-term burst of energy gained from a chocolate candy bar or a caffeinated beverage.

A better strategy, one that will allow you to keep annoying distractions at bay, is to set aside prioritized time for critical and important tasks. Then work through each task one at a time, giving each your full attention, focus, and concentration. This will also help prevent leadership derailment.

This strategy works best when you can ensconce yourself in a work environment (i.e. an office or small meeting room with a closed door) that prevents your fellow colleagues (and even your boss) from interrupting you. A good set of noise-canceling headphones helps as well, as long as the music you listen to is not distracting.

If you think this is taking things too far, remember this: it takes an average of 23 minutes and 15 seconds to return to the original task after an interruption, according to Gloria Mark, who studies digital distraction at the University of California Irvine. Even more disturbing (pun intended), her research also shows that a typical office worker gets only 11 minutes between each interruption.

Avoiding work disturbances and interruptions is critical for successful cognitive activity by leaders, and directly impacts the quality of decision making, thinking, and outcomes.

Pessimism

Pessimism is another common leadership derailment issue found within struggling leaders, at all levels of organizations. Pessimism is both a personality trait and product of a person's environment, especially during the formative childhood years.

Left unchecked for too long, negative thinking and pessimism can become a brain habit that can make you more prone to feeling overwhelmed, burned out, and mentally fatigued. It can also lead you to feel inadequate as a leader, resulting in the much-publicized imposter syndrome.

Ingrained pessimistic thinking automatically turns unknowns into negatives, clouding judgment and making it extremely hard to visualize potential benefits and positive outcomes. Decisions and actions are often paralyzed or postponed, usually in the hopes that new information will arise that will help make a choice clear cut. In the meantime, opportunities are lost and team members frustrated and confused by the lack of decisions and directions from their leaders.

Optimism is not just positive thinking or having a rose-colored glasses view of the world. Optimists tend to be realistic about the world and understand that there is both good and bad in the world (and in their own lives).

However, unlike pessimists, optimists look at problems with a solution focus. This is the defining trait of optimists. Where the pessimist sees unsolvable problems, the optimist sees temporary setbacks. The pessimist views their existence as an uncontrollable cruel fate, whereas the optimist sees the future as something to be created and optimized to the best of his ability.

Optimists see the future as malleable and thus work toward improving it. They take the steps required to best position themselves for being able to impact the future, including exercise, healthy eating, and nurturing mutually beneficial relationships.

Your experiences, thinking and thought patterns, behaviors, and habitual ways of reacting to the world around you (especially complaining) are inseparable from how your brain wires itself. Negative habits and thinking patterns change your brain for the worse. Positive behaviors and thinking change your brain for the better.

Complaining, especially constant complaining, is a harmful behavior. If allowed to loop within the brain, complaining alters thought processes and often leads to undesirable behavior. Pessimistic people are almost always complainers and when not voicing their complaints are most likely ruminating about them. Sadly, such rumination is linked directly to depressed and anxious brains.

In 2014, *Trends of Cognitive Science* listed the benefits of being more optimistic as improved career success, stronger relationships, protection against loneliness, and less chance of hospitalization after having surgery.

The impact of pessimism goes beyond workplace performance issues, workplace climate, and poor decision making. It also impacts the personal health of leaders.

A Finnish study reported that the most pessimistic men were four times as likely to develop coronary heart disease over a 10-year period as the least pessimistic men. And a Harvard research study pegged a pessimist's odds of developing heart disease at more than double that of an optimist.

A study of nearly 7000 students entering the University of North Carolina in the mid-1960s began with participants undergoing comprehensive personality testing to determine their outlook. These participants were tracked for over 40 years, during which 476 of them died. The most pessimistic segment of the study had a 42% higher death rate than the most optimistic group. The bottom line result: pessimists died younger.

A large study conducted by the Harvard School of Public Health found similar results. In this study, the most optimistic women were 30% less likely to die from any of the serious illnesses tracked during the 8 years of the study. This included fewer deaths from cancer, heart disease, and stroke.

Fortunately, several research studies have shown that optimism is definitely a learned trait. There are many ways to adopt an optimistic mindset, even for those who have been pessimists for most of their lives. By using the mindfulness techniques in this book (chapter 14) and other methods for consciously altering your thought processes, you can literally re-wire your brain to be more optimistic.

All of these leadership derailment issues negatively impact the thinking and decision-making processes of leaders, as well as their interpersonal relationships with direct reports, team members, colleagues, and peers. Which is obviously a problem, since leaders are basically paid to make decisions and lead people.

The next chapter will delve into other factors impacting decision making and thinking, as well as discussing why *mind full* leaders often make bad decisions.

CHAPTER 3

Decision Making

Decisions shape our lives. As leaders, the decisions we make and execute also shape the lives of our team members, colleagues, direct reports, customers, suppliers, and even the communities in which we operate and live.

Fortunately, decision making is a skill. And like all skills, it is something that can be learned, practiced, and enhanced over time.

Later in this book, I will share with you how mindfulness can help leaders overcome and manage these decision-making related fears and mistakes. First, however, I want to share with you some other factors that can impact and influence leadership decisions.

Your Decision-Making Brain

Scientists are gaining a grasp on the regions of the brain most responsible for our decision-making processes.

A study published in *Cell* revealed that the time it takes for the brain to create an answer to a problem correlates with the perceived difficulty of the decision and the decision-making level of cautiousness. This study, conducted by researchers at the University of Oxford, was focused on the decision threshold, which is the brain's ability to determine the level of a task based on the perceived difficulty of the task. Interestingly, our brains infer the difficulty of a task based on the initial information available to it. From this inference, the brain assigns a specified level or degree of difficulty threshold.

Intuitively, this makes sense. One of the first tasks in any decision-making process is to determine the perceived difficulty of making a viable decision. What to order at lunch at a favorite restaurant? A pretty easy decision most of the time. What to order from a restaurant in Lisbon when the menu is printed in Portuguese? That's a higher level of difficulty, unless you are fluent in Portuguese.

This study revealed one very interesting aspect of the brain's decision-making process. This is that the brain makes an assessment of the difficulty of a task in one single event, based on the information it initially has. Hence, new information being received does not, according to this study, change the perceived difficulty threshold of the decision.

Thus, based on the information given at the beginning of a task or a problem to be solved, the brain determines and sets out a decision difficulty threshold in that first instant. This directly impacts how quickly or slowly a decision will be made.

It also means, in today's world of information overload, that insufficient information getting through to the brain at the start of the decision-making process may be turning relatively straight-forward decisions into more difficult ones.

A lack of quality information getting through to the brain raises the perceived difficulty threshold and reduces the ability to make quicker decisions, even when timeliness is a critically important need.

While the Oxford research did not look into how stress impacts the initial information received by the brain, other research strongly shows that stress directly impacts the prefrontal cortex, and thus is likely to impact the amount and quality of information reaching the decision-making regions of the brain.

We all know that emotions can hijack the brain's thinking processes. I believe it was psychologist and author Daniel Goleman who first described this as "emotional hijacking."

Scientists are now proving how this happens and validating mindfulness as an approach for preventing and managing emotional hijacking. The brain comprises numerous, highly specialized modules, which are used for analyzing situations and preparing reactions to them. It is the interplay between these modules of the brain that determine behavior. Unfortunately, most of this interplay occurs subconsciously and automatically.

In a process that neuroscientists call pattern recognition, our brains try to reflexively counter decision-making anxieties by narrowing and simplifying our options. This attempt to find certainty in uncertain situations leads to premature conclusions that are often based on previous successful approaches and which prevents more and better options to surface or be considered.

In a similar way, emotional tagging in our memories sends us signals as to whether or not to pay attention to something or someone and what sort of action we should be considering. Interestingly, neurological research now shows that when the parts of our brain controlling emotions are damaged we become slow and incompetent decision makers even though we retain the capacity for objective analysis. We all know how it feels to make poor decisions when we are being "emotionally hijacked."

Because some modules of the brain focus on gathering benefits and other modules concentrate on delivering benefits, they are often in conflict. Hence the issues people who are trying to lose weight face when they stumble upon the smell of freshly baked donuts. One part of the brain wants to gather the benefits derived

:

from eating the donuts while another module is sending signals to reduce calorie consumption.

While these modules are interconnected, they are not integrated. Hence there are many so-called captains in the brain trying to assert command authority. While some people refer to the brain as being similar to a computer operating system, this really is not true. It is more like a collection of smartphone apps all opened at once and clamoring to be used. Just as a phone can only operate one app at a time (with the rest running in background mode), the brain only operates one module at a time with all the rest eagerly awaiting in standby mode.

These modules can also create conflict in emotional behavior. For instance, while giving someone a tongue-lashing over poor customer service may deliver an emotional benefit of expressing outrage, another module will be signaling that an angry outburst can have negative effects on blood pressure and heart health.

Neuroscience research is now revealing that mindfulness practices and meditation can train the brain to be less reactive to emotional swings. These techniques can also help prevent the wrong modules from hijacking control of our brains and decisions.

In his book *Altered Traits: Science Reveals How Meditation Changes Your Mind, Brain, and Body*, Daniel Goleman describes a study conducted with Buddhist monks:

> *The meditators' brains were scanned while they saw disturbing images of people suffering, like burn victims. The seasoned practitioners' brains revealed a lowered level of reactivity in the amygdala; they were more immune to emotional hijacking. The reason: their brains had stronger operative connectivity between the prefrontal*

cortex, which manages reactivity, and the amygdala, which triggers such reactions. As neuroscientists know, the stronger this particular link in the brain, the less a person will be hijacked by emotional downs and ups of all sorts.

When you are better able to cope and control your feelings, rather than just reacting instinctively to them, the greater will be your ability to remain calm and reject emotional hijacking. And, of course, the less you are hijacked by emotional swings, the better decisions you will make. This is why the first decision to make is the decision to pause and become determined to respond, rather than react.

The importance of maintaining control over the interactions between emotions and the brain has long been a secret of success for those in high-pressure careers, from ancient Samurai warriors to astronauts and Navy SEALs. We are now at a time when this knowledge can be applied to decision making for all levels of leaders, in all types of organizations.

The decision-making processes of the brain are also impacted by the interplay of working memory and short-term memory.

Working memory is task-oriented. This is how the brain creates interfaces and connections between the various processors of perception, attention, and memory. Working memory holds the information and associations relevant to a current task.

Short-term memory, on the other hand, is a cognitive process that allows us to store information (data, facts, words, sentences, concepts, etc.) for a short period of time. Short-term memory is associated with chunking, a concept that says most of us can remember about seven "chunks" of information for a brief period of time.

:

When a task or decision requires a high cognitive load — the amount of mental processing power required to learn or process information — this puts a high burden on working memory. Tasks and decisions that tax our working memory capacity thus become harder to deal with. Additionally, too much information, or incongruent and conflicting information, overloads short-term memory.

In either case, the decision-making brain starts to cough and sputter as cognitive stress takes over. Indecision and procrastination urges arise. Sometimes the overloaded brain triggers an emotional outburst or meltdown. In other circumstances the brain defaults to relying on previous decisions and experiences, creating the "gut feelings" of how to proceed safely and securely, though not necessarily creatively or innovatively.

It does not take a scientific research study to acknowledge that cognitive stress interferes with creativity and innovation. We have all experienced episodes of mental fatigue caused by hits to our working memory and/or short-term memory capacities.

Fortunately, there is a readily available prescription for handling these episodes — pause, breathe, step back, take a short break, recalibrate, and then return to the task or decision-making process. Whether you need two minutes, twenty minutes, or even two hours for this mental medicine to work does not matter.

Unfortunately, too many leaders consider using this prescription to be a sign of weakness. They fear the hardness of their leadership shell will be softened if they are seen needing to pause and take a break. So instead, they chug on, often at a greater clip to mask their need for a recalibration pause, and rush headlong into making decisions under cognitive stress. Both their organizations and their own leadership personas suffer as a consequence.

Think of your brain in such situations as an over-heated engine. Like the engine, your brain needs to cool down to function at optimal levels. Take the time you need, if you want to make better decisions. Otherwise, your decision-making brain has no option than to produce less-than-stellar decisions.

After all, numerous research studies have shown that we each have a limited amount of mental energy available to utilize when making decisions and choices. Thus, it is critical that important decisions — especially those that leaders make impacting others — are made when mental energy levels are at full power.

This also explains why leaders will tend to make poorer decisions later in the day than in the morning hours. It is a concept known as decision fatigue and it is a common type of cognitive stress familiar to us all. There is a biological price to be paid for making decision after decision after decision all day long. The more choices made throughout the day, the harder each one becomes for an unrested and spent brain.

Similar to physical fatigue, the main difference is that most people, especially leaders, are unaware when they start to become low on mental energy. The problem is that an energy depleted brain looks for shortcuts to its decision-making processing. One typical shortcut is to encourage impulsive actions that have not been thought through clearly (sure, go ahead and send that email, what could possibly go wrong?).

Another shortcut is to take the easy way out and do nothing. This saves the brain from further energy depletion as the need to agonize over options is put aside, either for a later time or forever. Doing nothing eases the mental strain of cognitive stress, but as mentioned earlier a decision to not make a decision is still a decision. And it is one with consequences and outcomes.

49

:

Sufficient and quality sleep also influence the brain's memory and decision-making functions. A recent study from researchers at the University of Zurich states that depriving ourselves of adequate sleep may lead to riskier decisions (casino operators have known this for years). Even worse, these researchers concluded that sleep shortcomings might even prevent us from realizing the increased risks from our decisions.

Decision-Making Limitations

Bounded rationality is the idea that in decision making, the rationality of individuals is limited by the information they have, the cognitive limitations of their minds, and the finite amount of time they have to make a decision.

Created as a theory of economic decision making by Herbert Simon, bounded rationality really defines the various limitations encountered in all decision-making efforts.

Another limitation on decision making has been described by Max Bazerman and Dolly Chugh as bounded awareness. This refers to the well-documented observation that people routinely overlook important information during the decision-making process. This is partially due to the tendency to be overly focused on the problem or task at hand, combined with our natural inclination to give great weight to previous experiences and trusted information sources when evaluating options.

Decision making is a fundamental aspect of our professional and personal lives. Every day we make hundreds, even thousands, of decisions. Unfortunately, stress and other factors often lead good leaders to make bad decisions.

As you will see in the next chapter, scientists now know that stress impacts both bounded rationality and bounded awareness.

Another major decision-making limitation is fear. In fact, weakness in decision making by leaders usually comes from a place of fear. The most common mistakes in decision making are typically caused by one of these four fears:

Fear of Taking Action — uncertainty or doubt about eventual outcomes cause many leaders to put off making decisions. Often this is done under the disguise of wanting more information and data, a common leadership disease known as paralysis by analysis.

Fear of Making a Mistake — leaders who worry about making an easy decision operate from a place of insecurity. They worry about making a wrongful decision, particularly on something that should be an easy decision to make. Such insecurity builds upon itself over time, resulting in a more fearful decision-making process.

Fear of History — all leaders have made mistakes and errors of judgment at some point in their careers. Unfortunately for some, the fear of repeating past mistakes weighs heavily on how they make future decisions.

Fear of Judgment — concern with how they will be judged by peers, bosses, and subordinates. Such leaders also fear how they will judge themselves, fully aware that their own self-criticisms and self-evaluations impact their own levels of self-confidence, courage, and fortitude.

Leaders who are too focused on the past or the future are most prone to these decision-making fears. Being mindful, however, and bringing a focus on the present, can help prevent these four fears from surfacing and negatively impacting the decision-

:

making process. Leaders also have to understand that not making a decision is, in effect, a decision itself.

One aspect of the decision-making process often overlooked by many leaders, particularly mid-level leaders and supervisors, concerns opportunity costs. While leaders are deliberating, or being delayed by their fears and personal decision-making weaknesses, time is lost. This does not mean that decisions should be rushed. Far from it. However, it does mean that leaders need to be aware of their personal fears and hurdles they bring to the decision-making process.

Unconscious Bias

Another major decision-making limitation, and one which does not get adequate discussion in the worlds of business and commerce, is the impact of unconscious bias in the decision-making process.

Decision making is fraught with biases that cloud judgment. We often remember bad experiences as good, and vice versa. We can (and do) let our emotions turn a rational choice into an irrational one. And we use social cues, often unconsciously, to make choices and decisions.

According to Dr. Joseph Dispenza, author of *Evolve Your Brain*, our brains process 400 billion bits of information per second, but we are only aware of 2,000 of those. And, according to multiple sources on the Internet, the average number of remotely conscious decisions an adult makes each day is roughly 35,000. No wonder our brain looks for shortcuts for processing all this information and making decisions.

What is bias? Bias is an assumption about a category of people, objects, and events that produces a prejudice in favor of or against a thing, person, or group. Biases may have positive or negative consequences and stem from our tendency to organize our social worlds through categorization.

While a conscious bias is explicit, an unconscious bias is implicit. Both can impact decision making, either consciously or subconsciously.

Unconscious biases are stereotypes about certain groups of people that individuals form from outside their own conscious awareness. Everyone holds unconscious beliefs about various social and identity groups. In fact, unconscious biases emerge during middle childhood and appear to develop across childhood. One example of early biases most of have experienced is that girls who take charge on the school playground are labeled as "pushy" or "bossy," while boys who do the same are seen as showing leadership capabilities.

Unconscious bias is more prevalent that conscious prejudice and is often incompatible with one's own conscious values. Additionally, unconscious bias is more likely to be predominant when we are multitasking, working under time pressure, or tired.

This universal tendency toward unconscious bias exists because bias is rooted in the brain. Scientists have recently determined that bias is found in the same region of the brain (the amygdala) associated with fear and threat.

Biases are neither good nor bad. In fact, biases allow us to efficiently process information about people. In some ways, biases are merely mental shortcuts based partially on social norms and stereotypes. Having biases does not make you (or anyone else) a bad person, but it can make you a bad decision maker.

For instance, making a decision based on a conscious or unconscious bias goes astray when we make a wrong assumption about a person and then take action or make decisions based on this wrong assumption. To avoid doing this, you need to become

:

more aware of how your biases are influencing the decisions you make.

As Mahzarin Banaji wrote in the *Harvard Business Review*, "Most of us believe that we are ethical and unbiased. We imagine we're good decision makers, able to objectively size up a job candidate or a venture deal and reach a fair and rational conclusion that is in our, and our organization's, best interests. But more than two decades of research confirms that, in reality, most of us fall woefully short of our inflated self-perception."

Cognitive biases, which include both conscious and unconscious biases, impact the way we each see the world around us. This is neither good nor bad. It is merely an aspect of being human. The important thing is that by becoming acutely aware of our individual biases, and by understanding how our specific biases impact our own decision making, we can overcome them, or at least limit their impact if we choose to do so.

On the other hand, cognitive biases can make our judgments irrational and less objective. For instance, there is the cognitive bias known as hyperbolic discounting, which is to give more weight to the option closer to the present time when considering a trade-off between two future moments.

There is also the famous gambler's fallacy that makes a person totally convinced that, if a coin has landed heads up four times in a row it is more likely to land tails up on the fifth toss. This is incorrect. On the fifth toss the odds are still 50-50 for both heads and tails.

Unconscious biases directly influence our emotional feelings, which in turn directly impacts and sways our decision-making processes. We may think we are making rational decisions, but often we are simply rationalizing decisions based partially or majorly on emotions. As psychotherapist Kathleen Saxton says,

"We may think we lead with thinking, but fundamentally what we are feeling is a greater driver."

Biases are not limited to ethnicity or gender. How prevalent are biases? They go a lot wider than you might think, as this list from the website YourBias.is shows, and each of these 24 biases can impact anyone's decision-making process:

1. Self-serving bias — you believe your failures are due to external factors, yet you are responsible for your successes.

2. Anchoring — the first thing you judge influences your judgment of all that follows.

3. Optimism bias — you overestimate the likelihood of positive outcomes.

4. Pessimism bias — you overestimate the likelihood of negative outcomes.

5. Negativity bias — you allow negative things to disproportionately influence your thinking.

6. Sunk cost — you irrationally cling to things that have already cost you something.

7. Group Think — you let the social dynamics of a group situation override the best outcomes.

8. In-group bias — you unfairly favor those who belong to your group (however you define your group).

9. Placebo effect — if you believe you are taking medicine it can sometimes "work" even if it is fake.

10. Backfire effect—when some aspect of your core beliefs is changed, it can cause you to believe even more strongly.

11. Availability heuristic — your judgments are influenced by what springs to mind most easily.

12. Framing effect — you allow yourself to be unduly influenced by context and delivery.

13. Declinism — you remember the past as better than it was and expect the future to be worse than it will likely be.

14. Curse of knowledge — once you understand something you presume it to be obvious to everyone.

15. Fundamental attribution error — you judge others on their character, but yourself on the situation.

16. Halo effect — how much you like someone, or how attractive they are, influences your other judgments of them.

17. Confirmation bias — you favor things that confirm your existing beliefs.

18. Dunning-Kruger Effect — the more you know, the less confident you are likely to be.

19. Barnum Effect — you see personal specifics in vague statements by filling in the gaps.

20. Belief bias — if a conclusion supports your existing beliefs, you will rationalize anything that supports it.

21. Just-world hypothesis — your preference for justice makes you presume it exists.

22. Bystander effect — you presume someone else is going to do something in an emergency situation.

23. Reactance — you would rather do the opposite of what someone is trying to make you do.

24. Spotlight effect — you overestimate how much people notice how you look and act.

Why *Mind Full* Leaders Make Bad Decisions

The daily juggling of data, reports, email, meetings, decisions, and way too much information makes it difficult to cope and results in leaders running on autopilot. We see these zoned out and inattentive leaders struggling to lead their teams and team members, as well as themselves. Many are so consumed with firefighting activities that few realize these fires have been caused by the bad decisions and choices they have made. Thus the cycle of stress-induced poor decision making is perpetuated by the stress of course correcting for the unanticipated results from previous poor decisions.

No wonder so many leaders operate in a *mind full* mode. This is not good. A more effective method is to make decisions in a mindful mode. Fortunately, this is a skill that can be learned, practiced, and ingrained.

Leaders are paid to make decisions and to ensure the execution of their decisions. And to course correct whenever a wrong decision is made or unexpected results occur from what was deemed a correct decision at the time.

Leaders spend an exorbitant amount of time in the decision-making process, deliberating the pros and cons of multiple options, analyzing potential outcomes, and trying to anticipate or measure the probable costs and impact of their decisions.

In an interview published by *Inc. Magazine* (May 2018), Stanford decision analysis expert Michelle Florendo shared five mistakes people make when facing hard choices:

1. Spending too much time in the research phase.

2. Not giving yourself enough time to learn how to make great decisions.

3. Confusing the quality of the decision with the quality of the outcome.

4. Mistaking your options as fixed and binary.

5. Getting stuck in a perfectionism trap.

Despite their good intentions, leaders make mistakes. And, unfortunately, no matter how good the information, data, and analysis available, intelligent people sometimes make important decisions that are flawed, imperfect, and even occasionally unsound.

According to neuroscientists, leaders make decisions largely through unconscious processes called pattern recognition and emotional tagging. While these processes often formulate quick and effective decisions (particularly for routine and oft-repeated choices and determinations), there can be fallout when these methods are used for highly important decisions, especially when under stress or time pressures.

Pattern recognition and emotional tagging warp the decision-making process through self-interest, emotional attachment, unconscious biases, or misleading memories. The result: errors of judgment leading to flawed, specious, and mistaken decisions that often produce unintended consequences and generally fail to produce expected outcomes.

Our brains use two hardwired processes for decision making. First, the brain uses pattern recognition to assess a situation or the information available concerning a situation or problem that needs resolving. Then, based on the emotional associations (or tags) attached to any recognizable patterns, the brain helps us determine how to react (or ignore) what it has assessed.

This process of pattern recognition uses up to 30 different parts and regions of the brain to integrate and handle information. When faced with a new situation — either an event or a new problem to solve — pattern recognition helps us make assumptions and decisions based on prior experiences and judgments.

Additionally, the brain uses the process of emotional tagging to helps us determine whether or not to pay attention to something or someone. This process elicits and extracts any emotional information attached to the experiences and thoughts stored in our memories. This emotional information gives us clues on the type of actions we should be considering and contemplating. Unfortunately, when stress overloads and overburdens the regions of the brain responsible for controlling emotions and emotional reactions, the emotional tagging process is interfered with and inhibited.

When either of these two processes is impeded or obstructed, *mind full* leaders turn into slow and incompetent decision makers. The three main ways these processes are hindered and constrained are from:

1. Inappropriate self-interest — which makes us more willing and likely to perceive the patterns we want to see.

59

:

2. Distorting attachments — the bonds we form with people, places, and things can affect the judgments we form and the actions we are most likely to take.

3. Misleading memories — which cause us to overlook or undervalue critical differentiating factors that make the current circumstances not as analogous, relevant, and comparable to previous situations as our memories are leading us to believe.

Based on the way our brains work using pattern recognition and emotional tagging processes, it is not easy for *mind full* leaders to spot and prevent themselves from making errors in judgment and poor decisions. Leaders need to switch from *mind full* to *mindful* mode in order to make better decisions — based on better thinking — that result in better outcomes.

One result of being in *mind full* mode is the inability to control thoughts.

Having restless, uncontrollable, unpredictable, and fluctuating thoughts running through the brain is often called "monkey brain." These thought patterns can often hold leaders hostage, causing an unwillingness to take action or make decisions accompanied by fear, anxiety, stress, and negativity.

Why are leaders so susceptible to monkey brain? It comes from the constant, almost ceaseless barrage of decisions to make, risks to weigh, opportunities to scrutinize, people issues to deal with, and various other challenges. When the brain does not get a break from these never-ending issues that must be dealt with, it gets overwhelmed and besieged with a desire to enforce its own cognitive break. Monkey mind is the brain's way of fighting back when overworked and overstimulated.

Mindfulness is an excellent way to re-take control over monkey brain. A few quiet moments of calm introspection, or simply giving the brain a break by focusing on something peaceful and soothing, helps quiet monkey brain activity and thoughts. This will defuse the rhetoric cascading around your head and let you regain concentration and focus on what you should be attending to in the present moment.

Every business and every organization runs on thinking. Every leader makes decisions and acts as a result of his or her thinking processes. Hence — and this is very important in the information overload world in which all leaders operate — it is not just *what* you think, but *how* you think that makes a difference in the outcomes you generate.

As you will see in the next chapter, stress is a major factor impacting the decision-making process and the decisions of *mind full* leaders.

CHAPTER 4

Stress Leads to Poor Thinking and Bad Decisions

S tress is a major obstacle in life. A recent survey from the American Psychological Association (APA) states that nearly 50% of Americans are kept awake at night due to stress. And numerous studies have shown that cumulative and chronic stress are both linked to a higher risk of both heart attack and stroke.

Generation X (those born between 1965 and 1979) has been identified by the APA as the most stressed generation in the United States. This generation is now in the throes of parenthood, and one thing is certain — stressed parents are creating stressed out children. We might rightly call today's cadre of children and teenagers Generation Stressed Out.

As Dr. Kristen Race wrote in *Psychology Today* (April 2018), "Stress is both debilitating and highly contagious, so it makes perfect sense that a generation of stressed-out parents is raising a generation of stressed-out kids."

Stress in the Workplace

Congratulations American workers and leaders.

According to an annual survey by the American Psychological Association, Americans have set a new record for stress and anxiety. While the most commonly shared explanation for these high levels of stress in the U.S. is the nation's extreme political polarization, other factors include uncertainty about health care, medical bills, the cost of medication, the future of the nation, money, work, social divisiveness, the economy, unemployment, low wages, climate change, environmental issues, and trust in government.

In my work with leaders in Europe, Asia, Australia, and Latin American, I hear and see evidence of the same increased stress levels and a listing of the same causes (minus health care and medical expenses in Australia, Canada, and Europe — where national systems of public health care prevail). So high levels of stress are not just an American condition.

In fact, *The Guardian* newspaper reported that workplace stress costs U.K. businesses some £6.5B per year. While this pales to the estimated $500B per annum that workplace stress costs employers in the U.S., there is no doubt that workplace stress has a significant impact on profitability and productivity across the world. In many ways, we are all suffering the symptoms of the epidemic of stress sweeping the world today.

According to the American Institute of Stress (AIS) website, "Numerous studies show that job stress is far and away the major source of stress for American adults and that it has escalated precariously over the past few decades."

As a result, leaders must not only deal with their own personal stress levels, but they are also accountable for monitoring and managing the stress levels of their staffs. Here are some of the statistics from the AIS website that make managing the stress of others so stressful for leaders:

- 40% of workers reported their jobs as very or extremely stressful.

- 25% view their jobs as the number one stressor in their lives.

- 29% of workers felt quite a bit or extremely stressed at work.

- Job stress is more strongly associated with health complaints than financial or family problems.

- Nearly half of workers say they need help in learning how to manage stress and 42% say their coworkers needed such help.

- 14% of workers had felt like striking a coworker in the past year but did not.

- 25% have felt like screaming or shouting because of job stress.

- 10% are concerned about an individual at work they fear could become violent.

- 18% had experienced some sort of threat or verbal intimidation in the past year.

- 14% said they worked where machinery or equipment has been damaged because of workplace rage.

- 19% had quit a previous position because of job stress.

- Almost 25% had been driven to tears because of workplace stress.

No wonder Generation X was identified by the American Psychological Association as the most stressed generation in America. They now form the bulk of the workforce, and thus are experiencing the kinds of workplace stress cited by AIS in the above statistics.

We all know that being close to someone who is in a foul mood can result in our own disposition souring. And leaders know all too well that their own negative dispositions and moods can directly and indirectly impact direct reports, team members, and colleagues. We are now learning that the same may be true for stress.

A study published in *Nature Neuroscience* showed that stress may be contagious and that even the effect of stress on the brain may be transferable to others. While this study was conducted on mice, what is initially proven in mice is often later confirmed in human beings.

In this study, mice were exposed to mild stress and then returned to their partner. The most remarkable result of this experiment was that the neurons in the mice not exposed to the stress were altered in the exact same way as their partners who had been exposed.

While again this has not been scientifically proven in humans, leaders would be well advised to use mindfulness techniques to control and reduce their own stress, rather than exposing their stressful states to others in the workplace.

Impact of Stress

As athletes are well aware, peak performance can be activated through moderate and short-term periods of stress. Thus, feeling slightly nervous and anxious about an important presentation can actually prompt better performance. Hence, as long as stress is not experienced for lengthy periods, it is generally harmless, and can even be beneficial.

The same is not true for prolonged periods of stress or moments when stress levels are at extremely elevated levels. In addition to increasing the risk of heart disease, depression, hypertension, and obesity, this kind of stress decreases cognitive performance. This impact can affect memory recall and cause disruptions to a person's decision-making processes.

When we are exposed to long periods of stress (as many leaders are today), increased levels of glucose and fatty acids in our blood significantly raise the risk of cardiovascular disease and diabetes. A study at University College London concluded that stress also raises cholesterol levels, another known factor that increases the risk of cardiovascular disease.

In fact, stress can have major negative effects on our bodies, minds, emotions, and behavior as well. Here's a short summary of some of the major negative impacts of stress:

Body
Fatigue and general tiredness

Headaches

Frequent infections

Muscle tightness

Breathing difficulties

Skin irritations

Involuntary muscle twitching

Mind
Increased periods of worry

Increased procrastination

Impaired judgment

Reduced self-control

Inability to make decisions

Making hasty decisions without forethought and contemplation

Nightmares and bad dreams

Muddled, foggy thinking

Lack of clarity

Inability to focus or concentrate

Emotions
Apathy

Irritability

Quick to anger

Depression

Negativity

Moodiness

Alienation and social withdrawal

Apprehension, nervousness

Behavior
Loss of appetite or binge eating

Decreased libido

Increased alcohol consumption, alcohol abuse

Sleep difficulties, including insomnia

More frequent smoking

Accident prone, carelessness

The effects of constant and chronic stress are well known. In his book *The Happiness Handbook*, Dr. David Lee cites Robert Sapolsky, a professor of biological sciences and an authority on stress at Stanford University, in explaining how stress impacts our bodies. "In fight-or-flight mode, your body turns off all the long-term building and repair projects," explains Sapolsky. "Constant high levels of cortisol take your body's eye off the ball. Memory and accuracy are both impaired. Patrols for invaders aren't sent out, you tire more easily, you become depressed and reproduction gets downgraded."

Interestingly, our bodies are so wired and attuned to stress, because it is our internal mechanism for keeping us safe, that our systems do not differentiate between real and imagined stress triggers. That is why when we are worrying about a future event, or ruminating excessively about something from the past, our bodies produce the same hormones like adrenal cortisol that they would if we were facing an actual physical threat such as a mugging scenario.

Thus, even though no physical or other real-life stress-inducing factors are present, your body will produce these hormones when you are feeling anxious or feeling fearful about a decision you need to make or an action you need to take. The secretion of these "fight or flight" hormones into your blood in turn trigger secretions in the brain not conducive to clear-headed thinking, judgment, and decision making.

Inflammation is the defensive response of the body's immune system to threats such as an infection or a strained muscle. Scientists now know that stress can also cause an increase of inflammation within the body, much like an infection or a turned ankle. This inflammatory response to stress also impacts how the brain functions cognitively and how it regulates emotional response.

There are other ways that stress impacts our bodies, many of which are warning signs of intense or prolonged periods of stress. These include bad breath, sore or bleeding gums, sore and tense muscles, heavy breathing through the mouth, and an appetite that is never fully satisfied. Weirdly, stress can also make you not want to eat at all (we each react to stress in our own ways). Similarly, both diarrhea and constipation can result from stress.

In addition, having adrenal cortisol coursing through the body in response to stress depresses the immune system. This can lead to feelings of being burnt out and exhausted, which in turns leads to further stress. To say the least, stress is a very nasty cycle impacting our bodies, brains, emotions, and thoughts.

Stress also tends to negatively impact our sleep cycles. One might think that feeling burned out and exhausted would result in a greater propensity for sleep. And sometimes it does, for a few days. Unfortunately, this type of sleep often leaves us more lethargic and de-energized than before, which again induces more stress. As above, it is a vicious cycle.

But the most common impact of stress on quality sleep is insomnia, a condition that includes trouble getting to sleep and/or staying asleep. Stress can hinder your ability to wind down and get to sleep. It can also cause a series of racing thoughts that prevents your mind from shutting down and granting you the deep sleep you so rightly deserve. To say the least, the connection between sleep and stress is a complicated and highly integrated relationship.

Prolonged daily stress, and the resultant production and accumulation of adrenal cortisol in your body, also impacts your digestion system and metabolism, including your body's ability to absorb nutrients. Additionally, stress can cause your esophagus to go into spasm, increase stomach acid making you feel nauseous, affect the contractions of your digestive system, and even decrease the secretions needed for proper digestion.

The physical effects of stress include weight change, elevated blood pressure, indigestion, and inflammation. And adrenal fatigue from too many stress-fighting hormones rushing through your system is a cause of the mental effects of stress such as moodiness, irritability, and brain fog.

Interestingly, some of the so-called productivity tools we bring into our lives actually increase our stress levels instead of decreasing them. Smartphones are just one great example. The constant availability to check email and social media updates reduces our opportunities to switch off and give our brains a break.

Additionally, all the buzzes, bings, chimes, and other electronic noise notifications jolt our stress hormones into action similar to more dire fight-or-flight situations. Notice your reactions the next time your smartphone tells you there is something "important" for you to look at. Chances are, if you pause long enough to notice instead of instinctively reaching for your mobile device, you will likely detect a slight change in your breathing pattern, a quicker heartbeat, muscles contracting or tightening, a rumble of unease in the gastrointestinal area, or even some slight perspiration forming in your palms or above your eyes.

Are any of these physical disturbances, albeit as slight as they may be, worth the constant whirl of notifications? And, while small in nature, what will be the cumulative effect of these physical reactions over time on your overall health and wellbeing?

71

:

There is simply no need to live a life constantly tethered to a mobile device. At a minimum, turn off those social media notifications. When possible — and it is definitely possible — switch your mobile devices to airplane mode for an hour or two a day. You will be amazed at how refreshed and calm you feel during these mobile device sabbatical periods.

In an article in the *Australian Financial Review* (March 11, 2018), endocrinologist Robert Lustig of the University of California San Francisco says that, "Notifications from our phones are training our brains to be in a nearly constant state of stress and fear by establishing a stress-fear memory pathway. And such a state means that the prefrontal cortex, the part of our brains that normally deal with some of our highest-order cognitive functioning, goes completely haywire, and basically shuts down."

Impact of Stress on the Brain

There is a greater increase in cognitive stress in leaders than ever before, mostly as a result of information overload combined with an ever-increasing array of distractions and interruptions. Leaders need to take a collective deep breath, pause, and regain control of their reactionary minds.

An article in the *Harvard Business Review* (Feb 2009) indicates the brain is wired to be more reactionary under stress.

In fact, this flight-or-flight wiring results in stressed-out leaders falling prey to binary choice decision making, which limits the options they take into consideration. As Ron Carucci writes in a subsequent *Harvard Business Review* (August 2017) article, "In tough moments, we reach for premature conclusions rather than opening ourselves to more and better options."

Carucci goes on to conclude that, "Faced with less familiar conditions for which our tried-and-true approaches won't work, we reflexively counter our natural anxiety by narrowing and simplifying our options. Unfortunately, the attempt to improve certainty on the uncertain tends to oversimplify things to a black-and-white, all-or-nothing extreme."

It is obvious that too much stress is bad for overall health, and this includes the overall health of the brain. A study conducted at Yale University recently found that prolonged stress causes degeneration in the area of the brain responsible for self-control. That is why drug use and alcohol abuse sends overly stressed people down the slippery slope of self-destruction. Their extreme and continuous periods of stress disable their abilities to exercise self-control over their drug and alcohol usage.

If the stress experience is too overwhelming for the usual memory retrieval and processing of the situation, our brains instinctively shift to survival mode. In survival mode, memories and previous response patterns developed in reaction to prior stressful experiences can hijack our emotional and cognitive responses. This often leads to behaviors, actions, and verbal outbursts which do not fit the circumstances and which do not help to alleviate the situation. In fact, our reactionary actions, behaviors, and words often make the situation worse, thus increasing the stress levels for all involved.

Working memory is the short-term memory system that helps us remember things while we do a task, such as typing the URL address of a website or remembering our User ID and password access codes.

The working memory function within the brain has limited capacity, which means it can retain only a finite amount of information at any given time. Thus, if the working memory of the brain is absorbed in handling stress-related thoughts, there is less working memory capacity available to attend to the other tasks at hand, including making decisions.

If threat-stimuli information enters the brain's working memory capacity, it can exert a negative influence on subsequent thoughts, emotions, and behaviors. Again, this happens automatically and subconsciously. The antidote is to become acutely aware when this happens, and then take proactive steps such as purposeful breathing, reframing your perspectives, and preventing negative self-talk to take over (all techniques discussed in chapter 14).

Stress causes a flood of neurohormones to rush to the prefrontal cortex. These neurohormones impair the processing function of the prefrontal cortex, while simultaneously strengthening the emotional responses being generated by the amygdala. This also causes both the amygdala and the prefrontal cortex to change structurally.

At the cellular level, dendrites are the branches of nerve cells that receive electrochemical stimulation from nearby neurons. The rushing in of neurohormones created from stress stimuli causes atrophy in the dendrites of the prefrontal cortex and extension of the dendrites found in the amygdala. This leads to fewer neurons being fired in the thinking brain (prefrontal cortex) and more neurons firing off in the emotional brain (amygdala).

As a result, emotions override cognitive thinking, and we all know how well that typically works out. And, of course, poorly modulated emotional responses not only fail to resolve most stressful situations, they also tend to lead to more stress and more impaired cognitive functioning.

Not all stress, of course, is bad. Moderate and intermittent levels of stress produce adrenalin, a chemical that improves short-term performance and increases alertness. This benefits leaders equally as well as high-performance athletes.

In addition, research at the University of California Berkeley found that the onset of stress actually prompts the brain into growing new cells responsible for memory. Unfortunately, this effect is only witnessed when stress is intermittent. When such stress continues beyond a few months into a protracted state, the brain's ability to develop new brain cells is quickly suppressed.

How the Brain and Body Communicate During Stress

Research from the field of neuroscience continues to provide new evidence and clues on what happens in the brain during moments of threats and stress.

Functionally, the amygdala is the emotional control center of the brain, triggering and regulating the fight-flight-freeze response. Fortunately, especially when threats are perceived, the amygdala responds automatically and immediately. Unfortunately, however, it can also respond irrationally.

When faced with a threatening situation (real or imagined), the amygdala releases a rush of stress hormones (mostly adrenal cortisol) that floods the body before the prefrontal lobe (the regulating executive function control center of the brain) can mediate this impulse reaction. As a result, the survival instinct of the amygdala reacts before the rational functions within the brain have time to logically think through the situation.

Any strong emotion, such as anxiety, joy, anger, fear, and worry, sets off the amygdala and impairs the working memory of the prefrontal cortex. In essence, the power of emotions overwhelms rationality. This is why we cannot think straight or rationally when we are emotionally excited, upset, agitated, or stressed.

An easy way of grasping what is happening within the brain, and between your brain and your body, during times of increased

75

:

stress is to think of the brain as having four core functions. These core functions are the alarm and fear center (amygdala), the thinking center (prefrontal cortex), the filing center (working and recall memory), and the emotional regulation center (anterior cingulate cortex).

The thinking center of the prefrontal cortex is located near the top of the head, behind the forehead. It is responsible for a range of functions and abilities, including rational thoughts, problem solving, planning, empathy, self-awareness, and individual personality. When this section of the brain is in charge, we are able to think clearly, be aware of ourselves and others, and make good, decisive decisions.

Near the prefrontal cortex, but located deeper inside the brain, is the anterior cingulate cortex (ACC). This section has major (but not full) responsibility for regulating emotions. Ideally, it will have a close working relationship with the prefrontal cortex areas, but this is not always the case.

When the ACC region is strong, a person is better able to manage and control difficult emotions and thoughts without being overwhelmed and incapacitated by them. Basically, when functioning effectively, the ACC helps us manage our emotions so that we do not do or say things we will later regret.

The amygdala is a smallish structure located deep inside the brain that serves as our fear and alarm center. Because of its importance for our survival, this subcortical area is outside our conscious awareness or control. Its primary function is to receive all incoming information from our five senses (seeing, hearing, smelling, touching, and tasting) and assess this information on one solitary criterion: is this a threat?

If the amygdala determines that a threat is present, it produces fear in us. The higher the perceived level of danger from the threat, the higher the fear level. Simultaneously, it also sends signals to the body to produce a fight, flight, or freeze response. All this is done unconsciously and automatically without our cognitive control.

Of course, communication between our brains and our bodies is not a one-way street. Our bodies are constantly communicating stimuli to our brains, as well as continuously providing life nourishing blood and oxygen flow. Here again, some of this body to brain communication is automated and conducted subconsciously.

For instance, normal respiratory rates for adults are 12-18 breaths per minute. However, this can increase to 20 or more breaths per minute when a person is panicked or highly stressed. The body's innate response to fear and stress through faster breathing impacts brain functions and likely results in faster response times to the dangerous stimuli being faced.

While this is great when the stress is caused by a life-threatening or serious injury threat (i.e. move fast a fire is approaching), it backfires on us in less dangerous scenarios. If the stress is causing an emotional outburst that the ACC cannot control, faster breathing simply hastens this negative reaction. The increased oxygen flow to the brain is merely speeding up the emotional hijacking and resultant behavioral response.

This is why rhythmic breathing (see pages 228-232) is crucial for helping the ACC regain emotional control and to enable the prefrontal cortex to take back overall response control from the amygdala. Doing so leads to better decisions being made and more appropriate emotions and actions being displayed.

When stress hits and our coping mechanisms are overwhelmed, the alarm center takes over from the thinking center. This moves us from normal mode into survival mode, due to the perceived presence of fearful stimuli.

The placement of the limbic brain, which comes before the prefrontal cortex brain region, means that our limbic system, or our feelings system, reacts before anything else. The vagus nerve is at the heart of the limbic system and connects the brain physically to the body. The vagus nerve travels from the back of the brain through all of the body's organs and systems.

The vagus nerve communicates to the brain how we are feeling. These feelings in various parts of the body contain information that is sent to the brain via the vagus nerve. Likewise, what we are thinking about will be delivered throughout the body by the vagus nerve.

This is why a leader may feel nervous as she or he is making a decision. In such a case, either the unease about the decision is causing a negative feeling to be communicated to the brain, or thoughts of doubts and a lack of confidence in the decision are being communicated to the body and thereby causing nervousness or anxiety to surface.

The vagus nerve signals any disconnect between mind and body through various physical sensations, including dryness in the throat, palpitations in heartbeat, and queasiness in the gastrointestinal region.

The interconnectivity between the mind and body is multidimensional. Yet it is all too forgotten, particularly in the business world. Leaders typically believe that they are leading rationally with their thinking, but actually what leaders are feeling is often a greater driver and determinant of their decisions and actions.

Impact of Stress on Decision Making

Feeling stressed changes how people — including leaders — weigh risks and rewards during their decision-making processes.

Interesting, when under stress people actually focus on the way outcomes could go right. When under stress, the natural tendency is to pay more attention to positive information, while discounting negative information, according to research published in *Current Directions in Psychological Science*.

This means when people under stress are making a difficult decision, their tendency will be to pay more attention to the upsides of the alternatives under consideration and less attention to the downsides. The disastrous decision-making around the decision to launch the space shuttle *Challenger* is an unfortunate example of wrongfully paying too much attention to the upsides and not enough on the contradicting downsides information.

Research has also shown that stress increases the differences in how men and women think about and evaluate risk. When men are under stress, they have an increased tendency and willingness to take risks. When women are under stress, they have a tendency to get more conservative about risk. This, of course, is a generalization and even though there is scientific evidence to support this conclusion, it is critically important to remember that each of us has individual tendencies and preferences that may or may not be in line with gender generalizations.

Other research has shown that the stress of disruptions can significantly impact decision making. Participants scored much lower on a memory exercise when disruptions and interruptions occurred. In a 2009 article in *Psychological Science*, the authors of this study also noted that when under stress while needing to make a decision we are "more likely to bear in mind things that have been rewarding and to overlook information predicting negative outcomes." This conclusion is in agreement with the study referenced above about the tendency to focus on upsides, instead of downsides, when making decisions under stress.

Under stress people are more likely to make intuitive and quick decisions, without really thinking through the problem or task. This is because our brains are wired to be reactionary, not analytical, under stress.

Additionally, a common propensity under stress is to resort to decision making based on binary choices. Thus, people under stress tend to limit the options available to them to just two alternatives, usually in an attempt to arrive at a faster decision. Unfortunately, this not only prevents more and often better options to be considered, this can also result in premature conclusions based on only a subset of all available facts and information.

Most of us fall somewhere in between the two extremes of the "just trust your gut" decision maker and the "paralysis by analysis" let's analyze everything again and again decision maker. In fact, most of us move along this continuum fairly easily, depending on the difficulty and perceived risks of a particular decision.

However, it is important to know ourselves, our preferences, and our default mode when it comes to decision making. This is because, when under stress, we are most likely to fall into our default mode and preferred decision-making style, no matter how easy or difficult a decision may be. This is why stress causes some leaders to freeze and incapacitates their decision-making capabilities, even for the easiest and most routine of decisions.

As mentioned in the previous chapter, we rely on a pair of hardwired processes for decision making. Using pattern recognition our brains assess what appears to be going on. We then react to this information, or ignore it, due to the emotional tags stored in our memories. While normally highly reliable, these two processes can and do let us down, particularly in times of stress or tiredness.

Usually, the more stressful the circumstances being faced are, the more a leader needs to explore a wide range of options and potential solutions. Unfortunately, while relying on past experiences may create a false sense of comfort and confidence, limiting one's options is more often than not a recipe for disaster and poor decision making.

Stress is an enemy of short-term working memory, which lets you briefly hold and manipulate information in your brain. In military personnel, this skill is known to decline during stressful periods like combat deployment or even field training. In a University of Miami study, researchers provided eight hours of mindfulness instruction to U.S. soldiers over a month during their pre-deployment training. The researchers tested the soldiers' short-term memory before and after the intervention.

In the soldiers who completed a mindfulness program that emphasized in-class exercises, researchers detected no deterioration in working memory. In a second group, soldiers who took a lecture-focused mindfulness course, memory scores dipped slightly. In the third group, the soldiers who got no mindfulness training at all showed the highest slippage in working memory scores.

By bolstering cognitive resilience, the researchers say, mindfulness may help prevent errors during combat. Civilians in high-stress, high-performance situations may reap similar benefits.

Additionally, many poor decisions are made as a result of leaders feeling stressed and insecure about their positions, their career trajectories, their own confidence, and even what others may be thinking about them.

:

There are tremendous pressures and expectations placed on all leaders, from frontline supervisors and team leads to CEOs and political leaders. As a result, it is hard not to have some stressful insecurities and occasional feelings of nonconfidence. After all, there are so many variables with which to deal. So many unknowns that cannot be contemplated. So many people questioning your decisions. And so many personalities to deal with, including your own.

Of course, we all have insecurities at times, thinking that we are not good enough or that we are likely to fail on a particular assignment or task. For leaders, insecurities can be quite overwhelming, especially given the fear that a failure might have a negative impact on their internal organizational social status or their future promotability. Here is what often drives such stressful fears of failure and insecurities for leaders:

- Need for constant validation and approval.

- Ruminating and dwelling on past criticisms.

- Lack of trust in others, particularly peers and superiors.

- Inability to accept self-imperfections and one's own mistakes, and a history of blaming mistakes and errors on outside, uncontrollable factors.

- Falsely comparing one's self with those perceived to be more successful, either within the organization or in the industry.

Inculcating mindfulness into your thinking patterns is a reliable way to control feelings of insecurity. By focusing on the present moment on a regular and frequent basis, you will start to:

- Accept everything about yourself, nonjudg-mentally.

- Move past the past.

- Avoid comparing yourself with others.

- Become more trusting of others.

- Find that the validation from yourself is the only validation that matters.

These benefits of mindfulness were best summed up by ancient Chinese philosopher Lao-Tzu: "Because one believes in oneself one doesn't try to convince others. Because one is content with oneself, one doesn't need others' approval. Because one accepts one's self, the whole world accepts him or her."

Another decision-making peril caused by stress is the tendency for leaders, particularly new supervisors and mid-level leaders to start (or increase) micromanaging. If this happens frequently it can have significant long-term negative consequences for their teams, as micromanaging is cited as one of the most common reasons why employees quit. No one likes to be micromanaged by their leader.

As you will read in the next chapter, mindfulness has been proven to be a skillful method for stress reduction and all of the many associated ills and problems that result from accumulated stress. Additionally, stress reduction through mindfulness practices is a proven leadership performance advantage that comes with the side benefits of greater happiness, health, and wellbeing.

Impact of Emotional Stress on Decision Making

Our brains are wired to react. It is how our brains have evolved, from primeval times when faster reactions meant longer lives and potentially more progeny. Fast reactions meant survival, plain and simple.

Unfortunately, this wiring favors the amygdala over the prefrontal cortex. The result is that decision making can be adversely affected by the overreacting amygdala hijacking the brain's ability to produce rational and complex thinking. Fortunately, such hijacks can be controlled with practice and persistence.

Our emotional state in a given moment actually influences what we see and perceive, according to a study published in *Psychological Science*. What we see is not a direct reflection of the world, but rather a mental representation of the world that is induced by our emotional experiences.

"We do not passively detect information in the world and then react to it — we construct our perceptions of the world as the architects of our own experience. Our affective feelings are a critical determinant of the experience we create," the researchers from the University of California San Francisco reported. "That is, we do not come to know the world through only our external senses — we see the world differently when we feel pleasant or unpleasant."

The importance of this for leaders is to understand that your varying moods will influence your perceptions and valuations of the people you are dealing with, as well as the information, opinions, and recommendations you are receiving from them.

Emotions are powerful. They dictate your mood and, if left unchecked, compel you to react instead of responding to situations, events, and people. Gaining control over your emotions will enable you to become mentally stronger and empower you to respond to situations, events, and people instead of automatically and emotionally reacting to them.

Fortunately, regulating one's emotions is a skill and, like any skill, can be practiced, enhanced, and improved through effort, patience, and persistence. Regulating, or managing, your emotions does not mean suppressing them. Especially if they are intensively and deeply felt emotions. Sure, if something is just a little upsetting, you can choose to ignore such a feeling and move on. But if you attempt to suppress strongly felt emotions on the pretense that you do not want to offend somebody, then you are the one most likely to end up hurt and wounded.

Unaddressed negative emotions do not get solved by themselves. The saying that "time heals all wounds" is definitely not true. Time may heal some wounds. But in most instances the passage of the time merely takes the edge and sharpness off acute pain. In fact, suppressed feelings and emotions usually lead to negative coping strategies, such as excessive food intake, alcohol, or drugs. None of these are good decision-making or rational thinking strategies. All three of them lead to greater emotional stress in one's life.

While it is important to recognize and acknowledge your feelings and emotions, it is more important to recognize, acknowledge, and deeply understand that your feelings and emotions do not have to control you.

When your emotions get you down, especially when you need a clear head for making decisions or complex thinking, the three best things you can do are:

1. Label your emotions. Labeling how you are feeling can take a lot of the heat and hurt out of the emotion. Most important, labeling your emotions helps you to pause and consider how

85

these feelings may be affecting your decisions and thinking at that moment.

2. Reframe your thoughts. Pause and consider the emotional filter through which you are viewing a situation, event, or person. If you are in a good mood, is this causing you to misinterpret information too positively? If you are in a negative emotional state, is this causing you to misinterpret information too negatively? An email with positive feedback from your boss does not necessarily translate into a job promotion or a raise. Likewise, an email of criticism from your boss does not necessarily mean you are on the road to being fired.

3. Reframing your thoughts means taking the judgment out of them and developing a more realistic point of view.

4. Engage in a mood booster when in a negative emotional state. Take a walk outside. Occupy yourself with a few moments of mindfulness (see chapter 14 for a range of mindfulness techniques). Call a friend, family member, or even a colleague to talk about something pleasant (but no complaining!).

Another interesting revelation from recent research is that when we are angry we apparently believe we are smarter than everyone else around. This tendency to think that everyone is automatically dumber than ourselves when we are furious and feverishly angry was discovered in 2018 in a research study published in the journal *Intelligence.* The researchers studied people with trait anger.

Trait anger is defined by the *Encyclopedia of Behavioral Medicine* as a "dispositional characteristic where one experiences frequent anger, with varying intensity and is often accompanied by related negative emotions such as envy, resentment, hate, and disgust." People afflicted with trait anger are more likely to be described as having an angry personality characterized by hot-temperedness, and are also more likely to actually get angry. They are also more likely to display signs of narcissism — believing their world revolves around them — and go into episodes of rage when it does not.

Leaders with trait anger are more likely to wrongly think they are far more intelligent than the people around them, and thus less likely to consider the thoughts and ideas of others when making decisions. It is also harder to rationally argue with leaders who have trait anger as they are likely to react angrily to any comments or suggestions that oppose their views.

One of the best ways to prevent stress, especially emotional stress, from impacting decision making and thinking is to regularly stop and ask yourself this one simple question:

In what situations and interpersonal interactions do I regularly find my emotions and reactions working against me and my best interests?

Truly understanding the answer to this question — and then taking proactive steps to prevent emotional hijacking in such situations and interactions — is a sure-fire route to better decisions, better thinking, and better outcomes.

The next chapter will provide ideas and techniques for reducing work-related and personal stress, as well as ways to cope and handle general emotional stress and anxiety.

CHAPTER 5

Reducing Stress for Better Decisions, Better Thinking, and Better Outcomes

I f the previous chapter did not convince you to greatly reduce stress in your life, I do not know what will.

There are many ways to reduce stress in your life:

1. Limit (or eliminate) watching and listening to the news, particularly cable television news shows. You can still stay informed, particularly if you substitute broadcast news with an app like Flipboard which allows you to subscribe at no cost to a wide range of media articles and video clips.

2. When news is constantly presented in dramatic, news-breaking fashion — as it is on all the cable television broadcasts — it creates anxiety, fear, anger, and stress. This does not happen as easily with print media, no matter how biased or one-sided the coverage may be.

3. Practice mindfulness by focusing only on what is happening in the present moment. Bring forth self-awareness, compassion, and nonjudgmental thinking through the mindfulness techniques described in chapter 14. Respond with knowledge, insight, and forethought to the present moment rather than reacting in ways that create more stress or result in regrettable emotional outbursts or inappropriate action.

4. Focus on what you can control. Even as a leader you are unlikely to have absolute control over everything, even if you are the CEO. Your boss may have established a hiring freeze, and if there is nothing you can do about this then let it go. Work and lead as best you can within the parameters given.

5. Seek support, but do not unilaterally dump your problems, woes, and concerns on others. Support is best when it is a two-way street. Share your feelings and thoughts with like-minded people who can help you feel understood and supported. This alone will help to reduce the stress you are feeling. Be careful not to turn these conversations into office politics and back-stabbing gossip sessions.

Other effective stress coping strategies are:

Taking long, deep breaths.

Short meditation sessions of three to five minutes.

Maintaining one's sense of humor.

Walking outside (sunshine and fresh air are two of nature's top stress antidotes).

Reframing thoughts or fears into challenges to be overcome or dealt with to the best of your ability.

Any of the mindfulness techniques found in chapter 14.

And, there is also my personal favorite: eat moderate amounts of dark chocolate. People who eat more dark chocolate are less stressed, according to two recent scientific studies. These studies report that dark chocolate, with at least 70% concentration of cocoa, can have positive effects on stress, inflammation, memory, mood, and even the immune system. Other reported benefits include enhanced neuroplasticity, which is the brain's ability to adjust and create new neuronal connections as we encounter, learn, and adapt to new things and experiences. There's more on the benefits of moderate dark chocolate consumption near the end of this chapter.

Purposeful Breathing

This takes us back to using purposeful breathing to regain control when stress stimuli appear and multiply. Practicing purposeful breathing (see chapter 13) on a daily basis, even for just three to five minutes at a time, can be life changing by helping to de-stress your life.

Practicing purposeful breathing calms the stress responses emanating from the brain during moments of elevated stress. Additionally, the more you practice purposeful breathing at times when you are not under stress, the better you will become at using this technique as a de-stressing and calm-inducing tool when it is greatly needed.

Regular purposeful breathing practice strengthens the neural pathways in the anterior cingulate cortex (ACC) region of the

91

:

brain. As noted previously, this is the area of the brain that helps us maintain focus and attention, think clearly we when are upset, and prompts emotional intelligence to surface in our interactions with others. Keeping this part of the brain healthy and strong does wonders for how we engage with the people around us and for how we can be more intentional and stress-reducing in our actions, behaviors, and thoughts.

Diaphragmatic breathing (or what I call purposeful breathing — see chapter 13) instantly stimulates the vagus nerve and lowers the stress responses associated with the fight-flight-freeze mechanisms in the body. Stimulating the vagus nerve through deep, purposeful breathing not only reduces stress, but it also lowers anxiety, anger, and inflammation by activating the relaxation response of the parasympathetic nervous system.

Let's look at some other ways to reduce stress, stay calm, and handle anxiety.

Stress Relief for Leaders

Across the world, mindfulness and meditation practices are becoming less associated with only alternative lifestyles and cultures. In fact, mindfulness and meditation are actually increasingly becoming an important part of the daily routines for millions and millions of people. According to TIME magazine, yoga is now practiced by 11% of Americans and meditation is used by 9.9%.

How will this increase in personal mindfulness practices impact the workplace? According to some, it has already begun. In a study of 85,000 adults reported in the Centers for Disease Control and Prevention journal *Preventing Chronic Disease*, "Approximately one in seven workers report engagement in some form of mindfulness-based activity, and thus individuals can bring awareness of the benefit of used practices into the workplace." The authors of the study cited activities such as yoga and meditation as having been shown to improve employee well-being and productivity. Their conclusion: "the high and increasing rates of exposure to mindfulness practices among U.S. workers is encouraging."

How important is stress management for leaders? The emotional intelligence service TalentSmart conducted research with over one million people and found that 90% of top performers are skilled in remaining calm under stress.

There are numerous ways to reduce stress and its impact on your body, mind, emotions, and brain. Some of these are useful in combating momentary stress or anxiety, while others are long-term practices that can help you control the negative stresses in your life and aid you in making better decisions.

As in all methods for improving one's physical and mental wellbeing, it is best to consult with your physician or other certified medical practitioners before employing the techniques and methods outlined here. Also, for the tips and ideas here that resonate with you, I encourage you to do further in-depth research on the methods, benefits, and any side effects before you start to implement them. This section of *Better Decisions. Better Thinking. Better Outcomes. How To Go From Mind Full To Mindful Leadership* is designed to serve merely as an overview of some of the techniques and methods I have studied and utilized.

Reducing Work-Related Stress

1. Understand the normalcy of anxiety. Everyone has moments of anxiety. Unfortunately, worrying about your feelings of anxiety only serves to intensify and prolong those anxious feelings.

:

Research shows that people who focus on their personal strengths and personal coping mechanisms (such as self-talk or recalling memories of past successes) in moments of anxiety can significantly decrease the strength and length of such feelings.

On the other hand, those who designated their anxious feelings as a personal weakness and deficiency actually raise their levels of anxiety and reduce their levels of self-confidence.

2. Stay connected with peers and friends. Networking, both internally and externally, is good for emotional wellbeing and quality of life. Many leaders isolate themselves, fearing that any inadequacies or self-doubts will be visible to others.

   Interacting with peers or friends is one way for leaders to allow themselves to be vulnerable and express their tightly held fears in a safe and trusting environment. It is also a great way to be reminded that none of us is infallible or free of errors and mistakes, which can help reduce the angst surrounding the tougher decisions we face.

3. Focus on priorities. It is very easy for leaders to allow their calendars to be filled by others, to get swamped by the minutiae of daily decision making, and to get derailed by urgent matters taking priority over important tasks. Unfortunately, crossing out 10 or 15 small decisions off your task list is unlikely to produce the significant results that come from one

strategic decision made after hours of focused contemplation and analysis.

Years ago I divided my to-do list into two separate lists, one of which has the 5-6 major priorities I am working on (such as writing this book) and the other containing my list of getting "stuff" done. That GSD list receives a greatly reduced prioritization in my life, other than when specific deadlines (like a friend's birthday or the payment due dates on bills) give them immediacy or urgency.

Leaders who delegate more and micromanage less create more time for the priorities in their professional and personal lives. They also carve out more time, and more mental energy, for contemplating the bigger issues and decisions confronting them.

4. Practice purposeful rhythmic breathing. As soon as your body starts to send stress signals (shortness of breath, sweaty palms, churning in the gut, overwhelming sensations in your mind) hit the pause button. Literally.

   Through purposeful breathing you can quickly calm your nervous system and regain control over your thoughts and emotions. Purposeful breathing can be done anywhere in the office — at your desk, in a meeting surrounded by others, while walking to or from a meeting, or during a quick visit outside to engulf some fresh air and a bit of sunshine.

   There are many techniques and methods for purposeful breathing (several of which we describe in detail in chapter 13). All of them focus on purposefully creating a rhythmic breathing pattern. None require you to take off your shoes, close your eyes (though doing so can help prevent distractions), or positioning your body in a lotus position.

The best thing is to find and practice a pattern of breathing that works best for you. Here's mine: breathe in slowly through the nose, filling the abdomen and then the lungs beyond normal inhalation; hold breath for a count of eight; exhale very slowly until the abdomen and lungs are emptied more than normal. Hold emptiness stage for a count of eight. Repeat five to ten times as needed to regain a sense of calm and control.

Practicing such rhythmic breathing throughout the day also increases oxygen levels. When the level of oxygen reaching the brain increases the brain responds by sending signals to the body that it can relax. Increased oxygen levels in the brain will also trigger the release of feel-good hormones (such as dopamine) that help to relieve pain and increase feelings of wellness and happiness.

5. Respond instead of reacting. There are major differences between reacting to a situation and responding. Impulsively reacting tends to add more stress, to both yourself and others. Reacting also usually results in the first thought or idea becoming a decision, which often is not the best possible solution.

On the other hand, responding is more reflective and helps to redirect your thoughts to allow the consideration of a range of options. Responding, particularly with the phrase "let me think about that," does in fact help create time for adequate reflection, analysis, and contemplation. All of which will make you a better thinker and decision maker.

6. Ask the right questions instead of making an on-the-spot decision. This is not a procrastination technique unless used in the wrong way for the wrong reasons. Great leaders excel at asking the right questions to help their team members determine the best solutions. Such leaders know it is better to develop others by asking the right thought-provoking questions than it is for the leader to have all the right answers in hand and to make all the decisions.

   This has five benefits for leaders: a) less stress by reducing the need to always have all the answers, b) increased empowerment of their team members, c) greater development of their team members, d) increased ownership and commitment to the solution determined since this has emanated wholly or partially from the team members, and e) improved business results.

Reducing General Stress

1. Do not negatively judge yourself, your feelings, or your emotions. Accept how you are feeling — tired, anxious, nervous, overwhelmed, afraid,

uncertain, etc. Accept the reality of how you are feeling, without judgment or self-criticism.

Pause and reflect on the likely root causes of your feelings, again without judgment or blame (especially without blaming others or events). Own your feelings as yours. Do not try to shift ownership to someone else (i.e. she's making me feel this way). Your feelings are how you are reacting, consciously and unconsciously, to a situation, the behavior of another, or to what someone has said to you or about you. As Shakespeare wrote, "It is neither good nor bad, but thinking makes it so."

Self-criticism for having and experiencing your feelings is nothing but an additional stress booster. Hating or chastising yourself is negative energy that stress, and many other bad feelings, feed upon. Objectively assessing what you are feeling and the root causes of your stress are the first steps to regaining control of your feelings and rational thinking. Doing so helps prevent the emotional hijacking situations we discussed previously in chapter three.

2. Write down everything that is stressing you. It takes less than ten minutes to do a mind dump of everything that is aggravating and annoying you. Writing down this list of stresses, both big and small, eliminates the urge to keep everything bottled up in your mind (thus freeing up much-needed working memory space in your brain). It also usually results in an immediate reduction in stress levels.

3. Give yourself a break. Your body and your brain both require frequent periods of brief rest. Neither are designed to run at "Mach Two with your hair on fire" for extended periods of time. (Kudos to you if you get the gratuitous 1980s movie reference in the previous sentence.) A good rule of thumb is a five to ten-minute break every 60-75 minutes.

   These breaks can be as simple as a quick walk outside to get some fresh air, or moving to a quiet place where you can do some deep breathing exercises and mild stretching of legs, torso, back, and neck muscles. When these breaks are self-satisfying, they not only re-energize your body and brain, but they also have the benefit of increasing your body's levels of dopamine.

4. Enjoy a laugh. Laughter is a powerful medicine, especially in the fight against stress. I often coach leaders to replace cable news viewing (a known stress factor) with watching a comedy show like reruns of The Big Bang Theory. Alternatively, 15 minutes of silliness on YouTube will lighten your stress load.

5. Make exercise an integral part of your lifestyle. When the body moves it releases endorphins that help reduce stress levels. Exercise also helps boost energy levels and reduce incidents of insomnia. The body holds onto stress in both the digestive tract and within tight muscles. By loosening those tight muscles, exercise and stretching effectively lower your stress load.

6. Focus on the bigger picture. Daily life provides numerous opportunities to be stressed out. But focusing on the irritations, problems, and annoyances of your day-to-day world makes these issues appear bigger than they really are.

   Thinking about the larger context of life helps put the daily rhythm of stress into better perspective. Yes, that flat tire you experienced on the way to work needs to be replaced. But at least you did not lose control of the vehicle, causing you to crash or hurt someone. In the context of what could have gone wrong for you and others from a blown tire on the highway, having to miss that "important" conference call is not so earth-shattering after all.

7. Incorporate meditation into your daily activities. We list a range of meditative practices and techniques in chapter 15.

8. Practice purposeful rhythmic breathing multiple times every day (see point four above under reducing work-related stress).

Staying Calm

Our focus above mainly concerned long periods of stress. Let's now look at managing our emotions and staying calm when stress levels are momentarily escalated, often due to time-sensitive deadlines or crisis situations that suddenly appear.

In such situations, stress may actually help us perform better. Many of us have experienced times when the pressure of deadlines forced us to concentrate better. As a result, we experienced the phenomena known as "flow," resulting in some level of peak performance.

On the other hand, instances of unexpected stress or too much pressure to handle may lead to emotional outbursts, impaired cognitive responses, and even physical ailments.

Here are six methods for staying calm and controlling your emotions when stress threatens to take over a situation and hijack you either emotionally or cognitively. You will note that several of these have similarities with the techniques described above, and for good reason — negative stress is negative stress, whether it is the short-term kind or it hangs around for lengthy periods.

1. An attitude of gratitude. Daily reminders of what you are grateful for builds a solid wall against stress. Research conducted at the University of California Davis revealed that people who spend time daily to cultivate an attitude of gratitude and thankfulness experienced improved moods, energy, and physical wellbeing. Researchers believe that such daily gratitude practices, including the keeping of a gratitude journal in some instances, lowered levels of adrenal cortisol, the hormone which is associated with increased stress.

2. Remain positive. Our brains like to wander. They also like to attach themselves to random thoughts, either negative or positive. Rather than allow our brains to decide which thoughts to focus on, we need to be proactive by focusing on stress-free thoughts.

    Usually concentrating on any positive thought will do, even recalling positive experiences or successes from your past. This comes naturally when things are going well and our moods are great. But it takes a concentrated effort to do so when negative moments and bad news comes our way.

3. Cancel the negative self-talk sessions. Spending more than a few minutes chastising yourself for a mistake, a decision that turned out wrong, or for not speaking up for yourself or your ideas in a meeting is a sure-fire way to entice more stress in your life.

   Ruminating on negative thoughts, particularly about one's self or one's actions, gives them more power to create additional stress for you to deal with. Additionally, almost all negative self-talk centers around thoughts and opinions, not facts. But continuing to internally discuss and reinforce these thoughts and opinions gives them the credence of facts to our minds.

   Clearly identifying and labeling negative self-talk as mere thoughts, and then separating them from the actual facts (i.e. you do not always make poor presentations vs. yesterday's presentation was not your best effort) will help close the cycle of negativity swimming around in your mind and help move you to a more realistic and positive outlook.

4. Focus on purposeful breathing. As discussed above (pages 91-92), pausing to focus on deep, rhythmic breathing will help to rapidly calm both your body and your brain.

5. Reframe your perspective. It is a two-way, circular interaction. Our thoughts can increase our stress, and stress can impact our thoughts.

No wonder things can spiral out of control so quickly.

While you cannot always control your circumstances, you can always control how you respond emotionally and cognitively (provided you do not grant control to stress and negative thoughts). For any stressful situation, start by putting things into perspective. Then ask yourself, "how can I handle this situation without over-reacting emotionally and with the full resources of my cognitive faculties?"

Just asking this question confirms that you are purposefully remaining in control of your response to the given circumstances and situation. Now, list how you truly want to respond emotionally, either positively or neutrally. Note the phrase being used here: truly want to respond. It is not about how you might feel you want to react. It is about how you truly want to respond.

Next, list what is wrong with the situation and what are the possible solutions or fixes. And remember to keep breathing, rhythmically and deeply. This too shall pass.

6. Tap into your support system. Very rarely do stressful challenges need to be handled solely and without help. Often, however, challenges become stressful because we do not have all the skills or resources to deal with them by ourselves and we are reluctant to ask for help.

   This is where seeking the help, advice, and support of colleagues, peers, friends, and family members kicks in. A key to remaining calm in times of unexpected stress is knowing that help abounds in the form of your professional and personal support systems and networks. We all have weaknesses, and often the strengths and skills we need to complement our shortfalls are found within others.

Dark Chocolate Reduces Stress

Now for perhaps the best news you will find between the covers of this book, especially if you are a chocolate lover. Science has confirmed what some of us knew — and many of us hoped — all along: dark chocolate can reduce stress!

Chocolate can also reduce inflammation and improve one's mood (I think we all knew the latter, but it is nice to have it scientifically confirmed). Of course, these results also come with the caveat that chocolate should be consumed in moderation since its sugar content and high-calorie levels can impact the risks for both obesity and diabetes.

Researchers from Loma Linda University had participants eat one dark chocolate bar containing at least 70% cacao and then examined their brain waves. Gamma waves in the brains of participants showed increased activity only 30 minutes after the chocolate bars were consumed. Gamma waves signal that the nerves within the brain are working, leading to optimum learning and memory. Based on these results, it may be advisable to bring some dark chocolate to the next training program you attend.

It has been well known for many years that cacao is a major source of flavonoids, the extremely potent antioxidants and anti-inflammatory agents beneficial for brain and cardiovascular health. In the two studies conducted by Loma Linda University researchers, this was the first scientific proof that flavonoids also have a positive impact on cognitive memory, mood, immunity, and other beneficial effects.

In another study, researchers at Columbia University and New York University gave a large daily dose of flavanols extracted from cocoa powder to a group of participants. During the trial period the participants reported improved memory and tests showed enhanced blood flow to the hippocampus, the part of the brain responsible for memory formation.

Eating moderate amounts of dark chocolate on a regular basis has also been scientifically linked to reducing blood pressure, lowering inflammation, improving sensitivity to insulin (and thus reducing the risk for Type-2 diabetes), suppressing appetite, better protection against UV radiation in sunlight, eliminating low-density cholesterol (the bad cholesterol in blood), boosting mood by stimulating the production of serotonin, and reducing stress and anxiety during pregnancy.

Perhaps one day researchers will prove that eating chocolate will improve our memories to eat more chocolate! In moderation, of course.

Handling Anxiety

Anxiety is another type of stressor that many people and leaders face. In fact, anxiety disorders are the most common mental illness in the United States, affecting over 40 million adults.

Anxiety interferes with the brain's decision-making operations, but not for the reasons you might think. It appears that people at risk for anxiety have lower activity in a region of the brain responsible for complex mental operations, according to the results of a study at Duke University.

These research findings also showed that people whose brains exhibit a high response to threat and a lower response to reward are more at risk of developing symptoms of anxiety and depression over time. The individual configuration of the brain has a direct impact on one's propensity to incur anxiety.

Hence, signs of anxiety and the stresses associated with anxiety impact the brain's decision-making functionality. However, these signs may also be an indicator of a reduced activity level occurring in the brain's dorsolateral prefrontal cortex, the brain's executive control center which assists in focusing attention and planning complex actions.

When anxiety strikes, even at moderate or low levels, it can seem impossible to stop the downward spirals of worries, fears, and self-doubt. In her book *How to Be Yourself: Quiet Your Inner Critic and Rise Above Social Anxiety*, Boston University clinical psychologist Ellen Hendriksen shares a mindfulness hack that can help you stay in the moment when anxiety asserts itself.

Called the 5-4-3-2-1 method, this mindfulness technique can be used any time you find yourself ruminating over particular worries or feeling anxiously overwhelmed. The technique incorporates all five senses in order to ground yourself in the present moment by having you name:

1. Five things you can see.
2. Four things you can hear.
3. Three things you can feel via the sense of touch.
4. Two things you can smell.
5. One thing you can taste.

The relationship between the quantities and each particular sense does not matter. It is only important that all five senses are incorporated. So feel free to mix up the above example if you want (i.e. four things you can feel and three things you can hear). Again, the most important thing is that you scroll through all five senses, using your powers of observation to get the brain to focus on 15 specific things rather than the spinning thoughts concerning your worries or concerns, fears, or anxieties.

Once you are firmly rooted in the present moment through this technique you will be in a better position to deal more thoughtfully with those worries and concerns.

Now that we have seen how stress leads to poor thinking and bad decisions, and shown you various ways to reduce stress in order to create better decisions, thinking, and outcomes, let's look at some facts and myths about our brains.

CHAPTER 6

Brain Facts and Myths

There are numerous myths about the brain, one of which is that we supposedly use only 10% of brains (a myth believed by about 65% of Americans according to a 2013 survey conducted by the Michael J. Fox Foundation for Parkinson's Research).

Thanks to technological advancements, neuroscientists and researchers now have more sophisticated tools and equipment to provide us with increasing knowledge about the brain and how it functions. These tools have also enabled scientists to disprove some of the rampant and common misunderstandings of this all-important organ.

This chapter will highlight some of the more interesting and useful facts about the brain that decision makers should know.

> Brain Power — the old saying that we use only a small portion of our brains (the 10% figure is frequently cited) is wrong. Research has yet to find an area of the brain that is completely inactive. Even studies that measure activity at the single

neuron level have not revealed any inactive areas of the brain.

Modern scanning technology shows that we use most of our brains, most of the time. Even when we are asleep. Not every part of the brain is firing constantly all the time, however. This would likely overheat the brain and cause massive damage.

While all brain regions are not necessarily all active at the same time, all regions of the brain are utilized to some extent over the course of a day, depending on the activities of the individual. Hence, within every 24-hour cycle we are likely to tap into all regions of our brains as needed.

Left-brained or right-brained — our brains function as one entity, not as two distinct and separate hemispheres. Almost all brain functions require the interactions and interconnectivity of both hemispheres for these functions to be executed.

However, each hemisphere may perform separate functions to execute a task. For instance, the ability to understand and express language occurs in the left hemisphere, while other aspects of language processing, such as interpretation, rhythm, and word stress, happen in the right hemisphere.

Brain size — the size of the brain is not linked to the ability to learn or to intelligence levels. Additionally, even though men have larger brain volumes than women, this does not mean that the two genders are not equal in their learning capabilities. The male brain is larger due purely to relative body size. Besides, there is a lot of variability in brain size, structure, and wiring between individuals of the same gender.

100 Billion Neurons — the estimate of the brain having 100 billion neurons has been repeated so often that no one is completely sure where it originated. In 2009 a researcher set out to count neurons in adult brains and came up with a slightly lower tally of 85 billion neurons. However, I suspect television medical shows and Hollywood movies will continue to cite the 100 billion figure for years to come.

Adaptation — the brain can elicit other areas of itself to compensate for a damaged area when needed. This includes the ability to adapt to injuries such as stroke or head trauma. Also, the brain can rewire itself if needed so that healthy neurons can form new networks or even modify existing networks to compensate for a damaged part of the brain.

Maturity — sadly, especially for parents and teachers of adolescents, the brain does not fully grow and mature until around age 25. Additionally, it matures from back to front, meaning that the prefrontal cortex (home of judgment, problem solving, decision making, organized thinking, personality development, and impulse control) is the last region of the brain to finish developing.

The older brain — getting older does have some brain benefits, including a better ability to judge

111

the character of people, greater ability to differentiate the nuances of language, and an increased capability to keep emotions in check.

The teenage brain — it may seem like teenagers are brain dead, but in reality teenagers have overtaxed and overwhelmed brains. This is because they are starting to make more decisions for themselves, school is becoming more challenging (as are their social lives), and more responsibilities are being given to them by parents, teachers, coaches, and others.

Additionally, since the brain does not reach maturity until at least age 25, the teenage brain is having to calculate an increasing multitude of risk and reward decisions, problem-solving solutions, prioritizing, planning, thinking, and controlling emotions before it is completely grown and fully functional.

A multitude of senses — in addition to the five commonly taught senses of sight, hearing, taste, smell, and touch the brain actually has 21 slightly different ways of sensing things. Nociception refers to the senses of pressure, heat, and pain. Proprioception is a sense of where our bodies are and the position we are in. Interoceptive senses include balance, hunger, and thirst.

Decision Making — 95% of decisions are made in the subconscious mind. While these may sometimes feel like gut feelings, intuition, or instinctive reactions, they are actually subconscious thoughts and decisions. Leaders need to learn to slow down in order to tap into and leverage this valuable subconscious decision-making prowess that has been honed through decades of subconscious decision making.

Information flow overload — multiple studies have shown that very high levels of smartphone and Internet use is not good for the brain. It is not just the amount of information swamping our brains, it is also the fact that constant access to information via electronic devices prevents our brains from pausing long enough to catch a breath and refresh.

There is even a syndrome now known as "Google Brain," caused by constantly searching for more information that exhausts the brain, erodes deep thinking, and saps mental energy. Without a doubt, our brains need regular short breaks from screen time and the buzzing of alert notifications. Personally, I set my smartphone and iPad to airplane mode several times a day, just to keep myself from the temptation of constant information access.

Mental stimulation — the brain naturally craves stimulation. But this is no excuse for instinctively grabbing an electronic device to check email or social media feeds. Good conversation stimulates the brain. As does thinking through a large problem or opportunity. As does mindful meditation. The more mindful the stimulation, the better for the brain. Distractions like mindless television viewing and electronic device checking are not truly mental stimulation.

Multitasking — the brain cannot learn, process, or concentrate on more than one thing at a time. From a cognitive standpoint, multitasking is merely the toggling back and forth between tasks. Doing so decreases the brain's attention span, processing speed, and memory functions. It also decreases reaction capabilities and speed, resulting in accidents, miscommunication, and emotional outbursts.

The brain is not always inefficient when doing several things at once, especially with activities that are routine and regularly repeated (i.e. you can follow a movie plot and simultaneously eat dinner without spilling all over yourself). But when it comes to higher order thinking, the distractions caused by multitasking can severely impact the brain's ability to stay focused on a single task. Plus, multitasking has been shown to reduce creativity, increase errors, lower the ability to focus on what is most important, and increase problems with sleep, memory, and stress.

Repetitive thoughts — the brain generates 50,000 (or more) thoughts per day. Many of these are the same thoughts repeated from the previous day. While this can be good when storing new information in short-term or long-term memory, it can be bad if the repetitive thoughts are negative worries or concerns.

Additionally, too much repetitive thinking can block new information from being received, which results in repeated actions and decisions. Researchers estimate that 70% of our daily thoughts are negative. These include thoughts that are self-critical, pessimistic, grounded in fear, and full of worry.

Fixed IQ — no one's intelligence level is determined and fixed at birth, nor actually at any point in their life. Neuroplasticity research shows that new brain cells continue to be formed well into our elderly years. Intelligence is a result of education and practice. This is another reason why developing people to their full potential is a fundamental aspect of being a great leader.

Intuition — according to research, intuitive hunches are a real thing. They are the result of the brain storing, processing, and receiving information subconsciously. It is suspected that intuition, or so-called gut feelings, are instinctive reactions and decisions that rely on past experiences and external clues that are oblivious to our conscious thoughts.

Memory — outstanding memory is a skill and like any skill it can be learned, developed, and enhanced through practice, repetition, and correction of wrong technique.

Mnemonics work — you can strengthen your brain's recall capabilities through certain memory-enhancing techniques. Writing things down helps to boost short-term memory, as does repeating information several times. Acronyms can help you chunk information for easier recall, such as a shopping list called BELT (bacon, eggs, lettuce, and tomatoes). These memory techniques work by creating connections in the brain, thus

115

reshaping the brain's neural network for better recall.

Always awake — the brain does not sleep, though sleep is good for the brain. When we sleep the frontal cortex and somatosensory cortex areas remain active, partially to ensure our senses are alert to our surroundings and any impending dangers or threats (i.e. the smell of smoke indicating a fire) are quickly and accurately recognized.

Sleep deprivation — being sleep deprived can lead to cognitive functioning resembling that of being intoxicated. Repeated studies have shown that after 17 to 19 hours without sleep mental functioning and response speed were equivalent or worse to a blood alcohol content (BAC) reading of 0.05. After 24 hours of no sleep, performance measurements were equivalent to a BAC of 0.10. In all states, a BAC of 0.08 is the maximum level allowed to operate a vehicle. Other research has shown that the cumulative effect of consistently getting six hours of sleep or less has similar results.

Brain training — becoming proficient at Sudoku, crossword puzzles, or online brain games does not increase the scope and capabilities of your brain. While you may become great at these particular challenges, doing so will not increase your decision-making, planning, analytical, or judgment skills.

Brain boosting — you can develop your brain by focusing on broader, more dynamic skills than puzzle solving. Age-related brain decline can be countered through learning new skills such as a new language, how to play a musical instrument, or even new hobbies that require innovative thinking and problem solving.

Sex — sexual activity may improve mental performance and the production of new cells in the area of the brain responsible for memory. Plus, a recent study revealed that older adults who were sexually active scored better on cognitive tests than those who were not sexually active. Sex may also reduce anxiety and depression, which aids in better sleep patterns and thereby benefitting brain health as well. Lastly, another study showed that having sex once a week can actually help you live longer.

Time off — your brain thinks better after a vacation (now you just have to convince your boss of this). The brain is not designed to work non-stop without a glitch. That is why downtime is so important as it gives the brain a chance to rest, reboot, and return to peak performance. Fortunately, there is plenty of scientific research to substantiate the point that vacations and downtime are important for mental processing.

Lightbulb moments — another reason downtime is so important is that it frees your brain to think creatively. This leads to more mental breakthroughs or "ah-ha" moments where the creative lightbulb figuratively flashes above your head. These sudden moments of clarity and creativity do not actually come out of nowhere. They are the result of your mind working in the background on an issue or an idea. Then, because the brain is in a lower, more relaxed state during downtime, these flashes of inspiration have room to surface and appear.

Meditation — there are many compelling benefits of meditation, many of which will be highlighted later in this book. In terms of brain health, research shows that meditation sharpens attention and improves cognitive functioning. One study even showed that meditation can help preserve the brain and slow down the effects of aging on the brain. Another study found that meditation can improve both concentration and memory, two of the most important elements in decision making.

Exercise — exercise has been shown to improve cognitive functions at every age. Importantly, regular exercise has also been shown to reduce the risk of dementia in those 65 and older. Interestingly, studies have also revealed that exercising prior to learning a new task increases memory and concentration. The causal link appears to be the increase in blood circulation from exercising bringing oxygen and nutrients to the brain while simultaneously removing waste.

Water — even a slight amount of dehydration during the day can lead to short-term memory loss, brain fog, and an inability to concentrate and focus. The brain needs to be hydrated and so does the body. Drinking plenty of fluids also helps prevent headaches caused by a dehydrated brain. The brain does not store water, thus requiring a constant and frequent replenishing. A brain not properly hydrated causes moodiness, decreased alertness, and a slowness in the decision-making process.

Alcohol — while drinking adult beverages does not actually kill brain cells, as once believed, it does damage the connective tissue at the ends of neurons. This is why people do not remember what occurred while they were drunk. The brain is incapable of forming strong memories when a person is drunk due to the damage caused to the connective tissues of neurons.

Mediterranean diet — this well-documented dietary lifestyle of those living along the Mediterranean coast in Southern Europe has long been known to support heart health. Now, this diet rich in vegetables, fruits, whole grains, and fish is also believed to help preserve more brain volume in adults. This makes a lot of sense, as the saying "what is good for the heart is good for the brain" is much more than just an old wives' tale.

Olive oil — a staple part of the Mediterranean diet, extra-virgin olive oil has been found to help reduce brain inflammation as well as activate a process in which brain cells break down and remove debris and toxins. This process fights against the buildup of plaque and neurofibrillary tangles, two factors suspected of contributing to the symptoms of Alzheimer's disease.

Introverts and extroverts — the brains of introverts and extroverts are measurably different. In extroverts, the dopamine reward network is more active than in introverts. In introverts, their reward networks use the neurotransmitter acetylcholine, which makes introverts feel good when they turn inward. This also powers the ability of introverts to think deeply, reflect, and focus intently on a single task for a long period of time.

Social interaction — meaningful social activities help to maintain and increase brain function. One study showed that the memory center of seniors grew modestly after two years in a program that engaged them in meaningful and social activities.

Laughter — having a laugh is good medicine for the brain and has a positive effect on the brain's functioning. Numerous research studies have confirmed that laughter fuels the feel-good hormones dopamine and serotonin to be released. A good laugh can also result in the brain sending out endorphins to decrease pain, improve resiliency, and relax tightened muscles.

Hypertension — high blood pressure also affects brain functions, since healthy cognitive functioning is associated with unobstructed blood flow to the brain.

Common Myths

A research team surveyed people from different backgrounds to understand how commonly held are misperceptions about the brain, which they call neuromyths. Not surprisingly, the general public believed 68% of these neuromyths.

More surprising, however, was that educators believed 56% of them and even those with some previous neuroscience training actually believed 46% of the myths. So it is pretty obvious that the new information being discovered about the brain from recent neuroscientific research is not cascading abundantly beyond the upper echelons of the neuroscience community.

Of the 32 statements given to participants in this neuromyths study, here are the 18 that are false, though these neuromyths are still believed by many:

- Listening to classical music increases children's reasoning ability.

- It is best for children to learn their native language before a second language is learned.

- If students do not drink sufficient amounts of water their brains will shrink.

- Some of us are left-brained and some are right-brained and this helps explain the differences in how we learn.

- Brain development has finished by the time children reach puberty.

- We only use ten percent of our brains.

- When we sleep, the brain shuts down.

- There are specific periods in childhood after which certain things can no longer be learned.

- Learning is due to the addition of new cells in the brain.

- Individuals learn better when they receive information in their preferred learning style (e.g. auditory, visual, or kinesthetic).

- A common sign of dyslexia is seeing letters backward.

- Mental capacity is generic and cannot be changed by the environment or experience.

- Children need to be exposed to an enriched environment from birth to three years or they will lose learning capabilities permanently.

- Children are less attentive after consuming sugary drinks or snacks.

- Exercises that rehearse coordination of motor-perception skills can improve literacy skills.

- Children have learning styles that are dominated by a particular sense (e.g. seeing, hearing, or touch).

- Learning problems associated with developmental differences in brain function cannot be improved by education.

- Short bouts of motor coordination exercises can improve integration of left and right hemisphere brain function.

Here are the 14 factual statements about the brain used by the researchers in this study, which was published in *Frontiers in Psychology* in August 2017:

- Boys have bigger brains than girls, on average.

- When a brain region is damaged, other parts can take up its functions.

- Normal brain development involves the birth and death of brain cells.

- The brains of boys and girls develop at different rates.

- The left and right hemispheres of the brain work together.

- Information is stored in networks of cells distributed throughout the brain.

- Extended rehearsal of mental processes can change the structure of some parts of the brain.

- New connections in the brain can occur in old age.

- We use our brains 24-hours a day.

- Circadian rhythms shift during adolescence causing students to be tired during the first lessons at school.

- Academic achievement can be negatively impacted by skipping breakfast.

- Learning occurs through changes to the connections between brain cells.

- Vigorous exercise can improve mental function.

- There are specific periods in childhood when it is easier to learn certain things.

Let's move on from facts about the brain to facts about brain health.

CHAPTER 7

Brain Health

The brain is the most metabolically active organ in the body. It requires ten times the fuel of any other organ as it has to run 24/7 without sleep.

Weighing around three pounds, the human brain is a marvelous creation, containing around 85 billion neurons and trillions of interconnections called synapses.

Throughout one's life the brain changes more than any other part of the body. It begins to develop around the third week of gestation and continues to grow and develop through to old age (as long as its owner remains physically and mentally active). Its complex structures and functions are ever-changing, as are its neural networks and pathways.

When we fail to ensure the proper health of our brain by not adequately supplying it with the essential nutrients, vitamins, minerals, oxygen, and rest it needs, this all-important organ falters, sputters, and operates in less than peak performance mode.

In fact, most experts assert that a majority of people have underperforming brains simply because we are not feeding it the nutrients it needs.

A properly feed brain is equipped to be used to its full potential. Additional benefits of a brain-healthy diet include better sleep, improved moods, increased vitality, more focus, and even greater creativity. Plus, you will be better able to cope with stress.

Additionally, as you age the health of your brain will be a vital factor in keeping dementia and a range of brain-related diseases at bay.

Of course, health is holistic. A healthy brain can only occur in a healthy body. There are no shortcuts to this synergistic state. You cannot build a healthy brain while neglecting the overall health of your body.

The corollary is likewise true. Neglecting the health of your body is a direct route to having an unhealthy brain, one that is incapable of peak performance, especially during times of elevated or prolonged stress.

Brain health is a lifetime pursuit. Unfortunately, teenagers, young adults, and people in middle age are building a lifetime of unhealthy habits that could make them prime candidates for dementia in their 60s and 70s. These bad habits include too much junk food and fast food, obesity, and excessive amounts of sedentary time spent in front of computer screens and handheld mobile devices.

Add the high-stress, hurried, non-stop pace of life without daily mental relaxation breaks to the above habits and you have a recipe for cognitive decline and increased dementia levels.

The Aging Brain

Brain aging is inevitable, to some extent, in all of us. But brain aging is experienced differently by everyone. It is not a uniform process. The rate of cognitive decline affects some people sooner and/or more than others.

While some studies show that a third of older people struggle with declarative memory (memories of events or facts that have been stored and are retrievable), other studies show that 20% of 70-year olds can perform equally as well on cognitive tests as 20-year olds.

General physical changes that are thought to occur during normal brain aging include:

> Brain mass — shrinkage in the frontal lobe and hippocampus, the two areas involved in higher cognitive functions and the encoding of memories. This usually starts between the ages of 60 and 70.

> Cortical density — the outer ridge structure of the brain thins due to declining synaptic connections. Fewer such connections also contribute to slower cognitive processing.

> White matter — myelinated nerve fibers that are bundled into tracts and carry nerve signals between brain cells. The shrinkage of myelin slows processing and reduces cognitive function.

> Neurotransmitter systems — researchers believe that the brain generates less chemical messengers such as dopamine, acetylcholine, serotonin, and norepinephrine with age. The decreased activity in these neurotransmitters result in cognitive decline, reduced memory, and may increase depression.

Broadly speaking, the thinking skills that start to decline earliest are those that allow us to process information quickly and to respond to situations and others. In contrast, the brain retains and continues to develop the mental skills associated with accrued knowledge throughout our lives.

Of course, as we age our brains do actually get smaller in size. This natural occurrence is called brain atrophy. It is estimated that adults in their seventies will annually lose about 0.7% of the grey matter in their brains and roughly 1% of the white matter. Importantly, though, this shrinkage varies from individual to individual, with those who are less physically active seeing greater shrinkage than their more active counterparts. Being physically active is increasingly being linked in research studies to better thinking skills and overall brain health.

Scientists continue to identify factors that speed up brain aging. Not surprising, the usual culprits of overweight, poor diet, lack of physical activity, social isolation, poor sleep patterns, and stress tend to head the list.

For example, one study showed obesity in midlife may accelerate brain aging by approximately ten years. Other studies have identified sugar, soft drinks, and diet sodas to be connected with speeding up brain age, smaller overall brain volume, poor episodic memory, and a shrunken hippocampus.

In another study, this one from researchers at the University of California San Diego, major stressful life events such as divorce or the death of a loved one may actually accelerate aging in the brain. This study focused on the cerebral cortex region of the brain and used MRI scans to examine the volume and cortical thickness in the brains of the 359 participants.

All of the participants had experienced life-changing events within the previous two years and had undergone previous MRI measurements five years earlier as part of a longer-term study. These measurements were analyzed with software capable of determining brain age. The results showed premature aging in brain cells, faulty immune system response, and some genomic changes not seen in the participants who had not experienced significant life-changing events during the previous 24 months.

Researchers are gleaning hope from the variations in which brains age. The hope is that this is an indication that cognitive decline strictly as a result of aging might not be inevitable. Previously, the increase in cognitive decline in the general population was viewed as a result of people living longer. This was probably partially true. But the fact that it is not necessarily inevitable or unpreventable has research scientists around the world excitedly studying how to keep our brains young and functioning throughout our elderly years.

The cause of retirement-related cognitive decline appears to result from a lack of regular mental stimulation. This takes a heavy toll on cognition functions and also speeds up memory loss and dementia, according to a study of 34oo retired civil servants in the U.K.

The research found that verbal memory, which declines naturally with age, deteriorated 38% faster after these study participants had retired. The study report concluded that "retirement accelerates the decline in verbal memory function" and that there are benefits to be gained from "stimulating work activities that benefit older people's memory."

In other words, when it comes to the brain the old saying of "use it or lose it" is quite applicable. The best preventative medicine for retirement-related cognitive decline is to interact frequently with other people, stay active, eat a healthy diet, refrain from smoking, and drink alcohol in moderation.

:

Speaking of smoking, heavy cannabis smoking ages the brain by 2.8 years, according to a study published in 2018 in the *Journal of Alzheimer's Disease*. The study is the largest known brain imaging study and included 62,454 brain scans of over 30,000 people aged from nine months old to 105 years of age. While many studies are showing some medical benefits from marijuana usage, this study throws out a cautionary note and is important as more states legalize recreational and medicinal marijuana smoking.

There is a growing body of evidence suggesting that people who experience the least decline in cognitive functions and memory all share certain characteristics:

- They partake in physical activity.
- They pursue intellectually stimulating activities.
- They stay socially active.
- They manage stress levels.
- They eat healthily.
- They sleep well.

This list of common characteristics in those with healthy brains really contains no surprises. Happily, they are all lifestyle choices that can be made and implemented with little cost. Hence the secret to long-term brain health has less to do with solving Sudoku and crossword puzzles and more with trying new experiences, engaging with others, and maintaining (or improving) overall physical health.

Scientific research continues to provide proof that we can change our brains and our ability to cope with diseases and age-related decline with simple lifestyle choices. However, if the lifestyle changes are not implemented as early as possible, and by that I mean well before the retirement years approach, the more likely we are to develop neurodegenerative problems such as dementia and Alzheimer's disease. After all, it is the trifecta of mid-life curses — high blood pressure, obesity, and physical inactivity — that increases the risk of dementia in later life.

The extent to which scientists can pinpoint the contribution of any specific lifestyle factor (physical activity, diet, sleep, social interactions, general activity levels, etc.) to brain health remains limited. So there is no number one factor to pursue. You have to make a proactive commitment to a lifestyle that incorporates many of these factors.

And there are many highly modifiable lifestyle factors to choose from that can have far-reaching effects on brain health. These include obesity, physical inactivity, excessive television watching or Internet browsing, chronic stress, high blood pressure, poor nutritional intake, and inadequate sleep.

The good news is that lifestyle changes have proven to work, for both brain and body health. A large study of more than 21,000 American adults aged over 65 found that the prevalence of dementia had fallen by 25% over the 12-year period 2000 to 2012. In their paper presenting these findings, the researchers suggested this decrease may be due to increases in education and better control of risk factors for high cholesterol and high blood pressure.

Studies such as this provide some optimism — and clearly defined roadmaps — for taking charge of brain health through the use of tools, techniques, and general lifestyle choices that are likely to improve mental function, strengthen heart health, and reduce the occurrences and impact of elevated and chronic stress.

Alzheimer's and Dementia

Alzheimer's disease is one of the fastest growing epidemics in the world.

Nearly 47 million people worldwide live with dementia, according to the Alzheimer's Association. This number is projected to increase to 76 million by 2030. In the United States, there are over 5.7 million people living with this neurodegenerative disease today. Shockingly, some estimates show that as many as 14 million people will be in need of full-time care for Alzheimer's disease in the United States by the year 2050.

No wonder our fear of having to battle Alzheimer's disease in our elderly years is so prevalent. It is a real issue, in the short term for the rapidly aging Baby Boomer generation and with near-term consequences for Generation X and Millennials, who will be in their 50s, 60s, 70s, and even 80s in 2050.

One of the main problems with Alzheimer's and other types of dementia is that they do not occur rapidly. Dementia is not like a heart attack that abruptly gives a person a wake-up call. Dementia is degenerative, occurring slowly over time. In that regards, dementia is a bit like weight gain — a few pounds here, a couple of added holiday pounds, a few more gained over time, and suddenly you are 15 pounds heavier.

Treatment for Alzheimer's disease and many other forms of dementia tends to focus on managing the symptoms — such as memory loss, agitation, and disorientation — rather than addressing the root causes. This needs to change now, by focusing on the lifestyle and brain health methods that are most likely to prevent or slow down dementia in all of us. Especially since numerous studies have proven that by keeping your brain active, maintaining cognitive skills, and exercising regularly can help ward off dementia.

Unfortunately, Alzheimer's is a disease that can be in the brain for as long as 20 years before you are symptomatic. This is another reason for making the necessary lifestyle changes as soon as possible. You are never too young, too fit, too mentally acute, or too smart to put off thinking about the long-term health of your brain.

No one is sure yet why more women than men are affected by Alzheimer's. However, it is suspected that hormones, and the changes that occur as a result of menopause, and the years leading up to it, during which estrogen levels start to plummet, play a factor. As neuroscientist Lisa Mosconi notes, "As estrogen declines, it leaves the brain a little bit unprotected and vulnerable to everything else. When women are in their 40s, their brains really start to look like they are aging faster than the brains of men who are exactly the same age."

Additionally, elevated blood sugar and pre-diabetes can double your odds for dementia and Alzheimer's disease.

Research by scientists at the University of Bordeaux in France published in the *Journal of the American Medical Association* studied over 6000 participants all above the age of 65. They concluded that there are seven lifestyle choices that increase the risk of dementia:

1. Smoking

2. BMI over 25

3. Not exercising regularly

4. Not eating fish twice a week or fruit and vegetables three times a day

5. Having high blood pressure (hypertension)

133

6. Having high cholesterol

7. Having high blood sugar

Interestingly, but again not surprising, following the Mediterranean diet reportedly can delay Alzheimer's disease by as long as three years, and perhaps even help prevent it completely. Several population studies have found that those who eat a Mediterranean diet — mostly plants, fish, and olive oil with limited intake of red meat, sugar, and processed foods — tend to be less prone to Alzheimer's disease.

Rheumatoid Arthritis

Over a million people in the United States struggle with rheumatoid arthritis. This autoimmune disorder occurs when the body's immune system does not recognize the synovial fluid in the joints and attacks it, causing chronic inflammation and pain.

A recent study at the University of Michigan found how the chronic inflammation of rheumatoid arthritis affects the brain and results in the symptoms commonly described as brain fog. Many people who suffer from rheumatoid arthritis report that their condition makes it difficult for them to think, concentrate, and even learn new things.

By looking at how inflammation affects patterns of functional connectivity in the brain, the scientists discovered through scanning technology that rheumatoid arthritis inflammation targets the brain and not just the joints as previously thought. They also discovered that this inflammation may actually be altering functional connections in the brain, thus causing some of the cognitive symptoms referred to as brain fog. It is hoped that further research into the links between rheumatoid arthritis and cognitive performance my lead scientists to develop methods to reduce or minimize the impact this condition is having on neural pathways and connections.

Neuroplasticity

Neuroplasticity refers to the ability of the brain to reorganize itself by forming new neural connections throughout our lives. Until recently, the prevailing view of neuroscientists was that the brain loses the ability to change form and function in the early years of adulthood. Research in recent years has turned this doctrine on its head and we now know that the brain retains impressive powers of neuroplasticity well into later life.

Perhaps some of the best news coming from the field of neuroscience are reports that scientists now believe that our brain cells continue to keep growing well into our 70s. A study released early in 2018 indicates that older adult brains can create just as many new cells as younger brains.

The focus of this study, by researchers from Columbia University and the New York State Psychiatric Institute, focused on the hippocampus region of the brain. Over the years, the hypothesis that neurogenesis, the production of new neurons, in the hippocampus stops as the brain ages has been hotly debated.

Earlier research had shown that the ability to grown new neurons in the hippocampus of primates definitely slowed with age. As this occurs, an area of the hippocampus called the dentate gyrus, which is extremely important for the formation of new memories, shrinks in volume. For years, scientists believed that this also occurs in humans, with the corresponding belief that if the hippocampus degenerates so too does memory performance.

By studying the hippocampus regions of recently deceased individuals, the researchers determined that healthy aging brains are capable of making the same number of new neurons in the hippocampus as younger brains.

Another example of this is seen in former smokers. There is abundant evidence that smoking is detrimental for brain health. For instance, smoking is known to thin the outer layers of the

135

brain, which are vital for memory, reasoning, and language functions. However, this thinning starts to reverse when a person quits smoking. Unfortunately, a full return to thick cortical layers is estimated to take approximately 25 years. So the sooner a person stops smoking, the better will be their chances of having strong memory, reasoning, and language capabilities when elderly.

Memory Overload

In 2008, a study from the University of California San Diego (called *How Much Information?*) reported that the average American consumed over 34 gigabytes and 100,000 words of information on a typical day. Two things should jump out at you from this data:

1) leaders are not the average person and thus are likely to be exposed to a much higher amount of information, and

2) in the decade since this study was done it is highly unlikely that the amount of information any of us is exposed to daily has decreased. So the corresponding figures for today are undoubtedly much higher.

All this information absorption and processing is taxing our finite short-term memory resources. This clutters our ability to work on tasks and make decisions. Cramming too much information into short-term memory clogs the brain. It is like having too many tabs open on a web browser, which slows down the processing speed of your computer.

But the solution does not come from trying to process this incoming information overload faster. The solution is to reduce the amount of unnecessary information being stored in short-term memory.

Trying to use short-term memory for long-term memory storage can lead to chronic stress, fatigue, and numerous memory recall issues. The challenge is to stop forcing your short-term memory to store data, details, and information you won't need until later. This would free up more short-term memory and information processing power to use for making higher quality decisions.

Memory overload often triggers a feeling of brain fog, a sensation of mental confusion combined with uncertainty, temporary memory recall issues, and a befuddlement wondering of why this is happening. It feels like a cloud has wrapped itself around your head, blocking your ability to think clearly and to process information as quickly as you normally do.

The important thing to remember is that brain fog is not the problem, unless it is experienced frequently over long periods (if so, contact your doctor). Rather, brain fog is usually a symptom of other underlying problems your body and brain are struggling with: insufficient sleep, enhanced stress, multitasking, minor dehydration, improper nutritional intake, and even allergies. The cure: in addition to a momentary pause to collect yourself (purposeful breathing and a short walk outside are top tactics), the best course of action is to correct these underlying root causes through better sleep, better stress management, drinking more water, eating healthier, and focusing fully on one task at a time.

Depression

In addition to stress, one of the leading deterrents to brain health is depression, which is more common in society today than most people realize.

Over 16 million people aged 18 or older in the U.S. had at least one major depressive episode in 2016, according to the National Institute of Mental Health. This makes major depression one of the most common mental disorders in the country.

The background risk for depression in the general population is about one in four. That means each of us has a 25% chance of becoming depressed at some point in our lives. And if your parents have been depressed, your risk jumps by a factor of three.

Fortunately, science is now providing proof that there are steps each of us can take to help ensure a healthy brain and reduce our own rates of cognitive decline. These steps are detailed in the next chapter.

CHAPTER 8

Healthy Brain Management

A few decades ago the health and wellness movement rose to prominence, fueled by a proliferation of books, videos, CDs, and experts espousing the benefits of aerobic exercise, running, walking, strength building, stretching, counting calories, faddish diets, and the importance of weight loss to ward off cardiovascular disease and other illnesses.

Missing from the voluminous array of information on how to improve our overall health and wellbeing were details on how to protect and boost the health of our brains. Technology at the time did not provide sufficient methodologies and means for research scientists to identify and link specific approaches to maintain or improve this three-pound engine that drives and controls our bodies.

Things have changed markedly in recent years as both technology and research grants have enabled neuroscientists to pinpoint the key factors impacting brain health. The top five methods nicely form the SEEMS acronym:

Sleep

Eating

Exercise

Mindfulness and Meditation

Stress Management

This chapter will focus on the first three: sufficient sleep, proper nutritional eating, and ongoing exercise. Mindfulness techniques will be detailed in chapter 14 and a range of meditation techniques will be overviewed in chapter 15, while stress management is discussed throughout this book and in greater detail in both chapter four and chapter five.

Not surprisingly, there is mounting evidence that many of the best steps you can take to improve the health of your body are also some of the best things you can do for the health of your brain.

Having a healthy brain, particularly into old age, is a lifestyle choice, as discussed in the previous chapter. In addition to the Big Five factors above, there are a multitude of things you can do to help protect or strengthen your brain, at any age. These include:

> Break out of your comfort zone. Your brain will stay fit and alert for longer if it is continuously challenged. Learning new skills, traveling to new places, and just being more curious about the world around you entices the brain to form new neural pathways and develop new connections. Even driving a different route to work can help take your brain off autopilot mode.

> Maintain an active social life. As human beings we are social creatures. But as we age, our social circles tend to become fewer and we typically engage in less social interactions on a daily basis.

This bad habit actually starts for many when increased workloads and job pressures reduce the time spent with family and friends.

Take five. The pressures of work and life, combined with unending information flow, means there is always something to clog or entertain the brain. But the brain needs to frequently reset. One recommended approach is called five-by-five: take five minutes five times a day to let your brain rest and reset. This can be a five-minute meditation session, a short stroll outside, or even five minutes of peaceful concentration on the sounds of nature.

Maintaining an active social life with friends and family is critical to cognitive health. According to a study reported in the *Journal of the International Neuropsychological Society*, cognitive decline was reduced by 70% in people who were frequently socially active compared to those who were more socially isolated.

Poor brain health is more serious than many people realize. In addition to being an important personal issue, brain health is also a major social health issue. According to the American Heart Association and the American Stroke Association, 60% of Americans will develop a brain disease in their lifetime. The two organizations estimate that by 2030 the total cost of Alzheimer's, dementia, and stroke will exceed $1 trillion.

In a scientific advisory published in the journal *Stroke* in 2017 by these two organizations, seven specific steps were identified to help individuals keep their brains healthier and reduce their personal risk of cognitive decline as they age:

1. Manage blood pressure

2. Control cholesterol

3. Keep blood sugar normal

4. Get physically active

5. Eat a healthy diet

6. Lose extra weight

7. Quit (or never start) smoking

The fact that these same seven steps also help prevent heart disease and stroke is no coincidence. As a bonus, these seven steps are also known to reduce cancer risk and protect the kidneys.

Research in the early years of the current century first linked cardiovascular risk factors like clogged arteries to Alzheimer's disease. And an Institute of Medicine paper in 2015 pushed heart-healthy strategies, like managing blood pressure and diabetes, as important ways to reduce the risk of cognitive decline.

The brain requires adequate blood flow to function optimally. When blood flow is slowed or blocked, because arteries are filled with plaque or the heart muscles are not pumping at normal strength, brain tissue and cells can become damaged. Elevated blood pressure, cholesterol, and high blood sugar can all impair or block the blood vessels leading to the brain. In worst cases, this results in strokes or mini-strokes, causing vascular dementia. In other cases, the constant squeezing of inadequate blood flow through blocked arteries results in a slowed, but constant, cognitive decline.

Belly fat is another important warning sign of future potential cognitive decline. Men in a Kaiser Permanente study who packed on the most abdominal fat by their 40s were the most likely to develop dementia later on in their lives. Fat cells increase inflammation throughout the body and brain. A combination of aerobic exercise and weight training is a proven method for melting away visceral fat.

In mid-2018, researchers concluded that having higher levels of abdominal fat in old age is directly correlated with a reduction in cognitive function. Conducted by researchers from St. James's Hospital and Trinity College Dublin in Northern Ireland, the study assessed more than 5000 adults over the age of 60 on a range of cognitive tests. Individuals with a higher waist-to-hip ratio, a standard measure of obesity, had reduced cognitive performance.

In analyzing their findings, these scientists concluded that the impact of excessive abdominal fat on cognitive abilities is likely due to increased secretion of inflammatory markers, particularly C-reactive protein. This chemical is produced in response to signals emitted by fat cells and have previously been linked to a decline in cognitive performance. Other studies have also shown that increased levels of inflammatory markers in the blood are observed in the lead up to dementia.

As referenced above and throughout this book, hypertension (high blood pressure) is also liked to brain health issues. A landmark study in the United States among hypertension patients showed that aggressively lowering blood pressure significantly reduced the risk of mild cognitive impairment and dementia. This was a large, government-back clinical trial involving over 9300 hypertension patients.

The study showed that aggressively reducing systolic blood pressure (the top number in a blood pressure reading) to below 120 resulted in a 19% lower rate of new cases of mild cognitive impairment (MCI) and a 15% reduction in both MCI and dementia. Reducing blood pressure has long been known as a critical factor in lowering the risks for stroke and heart attacks.

:

Scientists now know that doing so also supports healthy brain aging.

Dropping and maintaining a stable blood pressure is easier said than done in today's hectic world of pressing needs. However, high blood pressure deprives the brain of blood and nutrients. It is best to monitor your blood pressure yearly after age 40 and to develop a blood pressure reduction and maintenance plan with your physician if necessary.

Why should you make these lifestyle changes starting today no matter what your age? Partially the answer is because prevention is better than cure. Also, as Sandra Bond Chapman, the founder and director of the Center for BrainHealth at the University of Texas at Dallas, told the Chicago Tribune in early 2018, "Alzheimer's now tops heart disease and cancer when it comes to our fear factor about diseases."

Plus, as she notes, "Science is showing for the first time that our brain is the most modifiable part of our body and the easiest to strengthen, more than our heart or teeth."

Sleep

Although we spend as much as one-third of our lives sleeping, scientists are still befuddled as to exactly why. Our need for sleep remains one of the most challenging questions for the field of neurobiology to eventually answer.

No doubt sleep serves several important functions, for both the body and the brain. Neuroscientists do know that sleep is critical to support higher cognitive processes such as learning and memory. The restorative function of sleep definitely renews the brain's capacity to incorporate new information and to consolidate long-term memory, thereby incorporating new daily learning and experience with previous knowledge and experiences.

Insufficient sleep and periods of sleep deprivation have negative consequences for the health of the brain. The brains cells that destroy and digest wornout cells and debris go into overdrive in mice that are chronically sleep deprived. Researchers believe the same is true for the human brain.

While this might have some short-term benefits by cleaning potentially harmful debris and rebuilding worn neuronal circuitry, and thus protecting healthy brain connections, the long-term impact is likely to be dire. For one thing, a chronic lack of sleep increases the risk of Alzheimer's disease and other neurological disorders.

Sleeping too little is also a recognized link to attention deficits. Some research results are supporting a call for a possible reinterpretation of ADHD as a sleep-related disorder. Attention and decision making are abilities that operate on a shared axis in the brain. Thus it is not too farfetched to hypothesize and expect that something that affects one, such as inadequate sleep, would also impact the other.

A 2017 study at UCLA showed for the first time that fatigue disrupts the speed at which brain cells communicate. Additionally, the study concluded that sleep deprivation prevents memories from being encoded properly, and it also causes temporary lapses in memories and vision. It is little wonder that sleep deprivation and fatigue are the second leading causes of car accidents in the United States.

Importantly, this research study revealed that parts of the brain actually turn themselves off to rest even though the person remains awake for an extended period of time. This effect could, for instance, prevent a tired driver from noticing a pedestrian stepping in front of their car.

As Dr. Itzhak Fried, a professor of neurosurgery at UCLA told a British newspaper, "Inadequate sleep exerts a similar influence

145

:

on our brain as drinking too much. Yet no legal or medical standards exist for identifying over-tired drivers on the road the same way we target drunk drivers."

In the study, researchers were able to observe how sleep deprivation dampened brain cell activity. As the test respondents slowed down due to fatigue, so did their brain cells. Their neurons responded more slowly, fired more weakly, and the transmissions between brain cells dragged on longer than normal.

In a second finding, the researchers discovered that in the areas of the brain where the cells were firing and communicating more slowly, brain waves also slowed down. This suggested to the researchers that select regions of the brain were trying to sleep, thereby causing mental lapses even though the rest of the brain was alert and operating as usual.

A night of quality sleep resets the buildup of synaptic connectivity in the brain that accumulates during one's awake hours, according to a 2016 research study. Without the reset, neurons become so muddled with electrical activity that laying down new memories becomes harder. When given a memory test, sleep-deprived volunteers were much more forgetful than well-rested ones.

Interestingly, other studies have linked sleep deprivation to heightened risks for depression, obesity, diabetes, heart attacks, and stroke. Also, large population studies have revealed a sobering truth — the shorter your sleep, the shorter your life.

Eating

When it comes to eating, what is good for the heart is good for the brain. In fact, nutrition derived from food is the single most important factor influencing brain development and the maintaining of a healthy brain.

Diet-derived molecules, such as vitamins, omega-3 fatty acids, glucose, and numerous others are protectors and growers of healthy brains. For instance, glucose not only provides energy to the brain, it also enhances cognitive function and protects against Alzheimer's disease. Vitamin D is an important antioxidant used by brain cells and a deficiency of this vitamin is associated with an increased risk of both schizophrenia and multiple sclerosis.

The typical western diet, one high in saturated fats and sugars, also impacts the brain — and not in a good way. Not only is this eating pattern a cause of hypertension, cholesterol, and diabetes, it also affects the parts of the brain that are important for memory. It is also highly self-serving as it influences the part of the brain that makes people more likely to crave unhealthy food choices. In effect, it creates a vicious cycle with downward health consequences for both body and brain.

The evidence that poor food choices are weakening our brains grows every year. Research from the Cambridge Center for Aging and Neuroscience in the U.K. revealed that obese people have less white matter in their brains than lean people, effectively making their brains appear 10 years older. And research from the University of Arizona lends support to the theory that high body mass is linked to inflammation, which in turn affects the brain.

In a scientific breakthrough in 2017, an RMIT scientist in Australia showed that high-sugar diets in rats can alter decision making and the ability to control behavior. The next step is to show the same causal relationship in humans.

In the RMIT study, the scientist discovered that rats fed on high sugar diets suffered a loss of a type of neuron known as willpower neurons, part of a network of neurons called inhibitory neural circuits. Located throughout the brain, the inhibitory neural circuits are concentrated in the parts of the brain involved in decision making, impulse control, and delaying gratification (hence the nickname of willpower neurons).

In another study, which examined MRI brain scans of 330 cognitively normal adults, eating foods that raise inflammation in the body, such as sweets, fatty food, processed foods, and fried food, raises the risk of a shrinking or aging brain. This type of food consumption also raises the risk of having lower cognitive functions.

Research published in the journal *Science Translational Medicine* by researchers at the University of California San Diego in 2018 revealed that high-fat diets may impair the brain's ability to detect the hormone leptin, causing a condition called leptin resistance. Leptin is known as the energy expenditure hormone and is released as a signal to stop eating.

Leptin resistance occurs when the body is unable to read the signals that typically curb appetite. In effect, the body no longer knows whether it is hungry or not, and thus people with leptin resistance continue eating beyond the point of hunger satiation. Obesity is frequently characterized by leptin resistance.

Without a doubt, scientific research has proven that the so-called Mediterranean diet to be the most healthy eating regime for both body and brain. Actually, this plant-based consumption formula is more of an eating lifestyle than a true diet.

Named for the typical meals consumed by residents of the Mediterranean coastline, this eating plan incorporates fruits and vegetables into most meals, accompanied by whole grains, beans, nuts, seeds, fish, poultry, and olive oil. Absent are the staples of the typical western diet: refined flour, sugar, fats other than olive oil and omega-3 fats from fish, and a high intake of red meat. Moderate consumption of eggs and dairy is also included.

In a 2017 study of almost 1000 people by researchers at the University of Edinburgh in Scotland, elderly adults who followed the Mediterranean diet principles more closely were less likely to lose total brain volume over a three year period. Other studies have shown that consuming extra-virgin olive oil can protect memory and learning ability.

These Mediterranean-style eating practices have long been linked by researchers to stronger bones, healthier hearts, reduced blood pressure, less risk for diabetes, and a longer life. Now research is showing that this eating style can also lower the risk for dementia by around 30% to 35%.

Martha Clare Morris, a nutritional epidemiologist at Rush Medical Center in Chicago, has taken the approach to a healthy brain diet a step further. She created the MIND diet, which combines the best brain foods of the Mediterranean diet with the famous salt-reducing DASH diet. The DASH (Dietary Approach to Stop Hypertension) eating plan resulted from study results published in 1997 and is the diet recommended by the National Heart, Lung and Blood Institute (part of the National Institute of Health) for lowering blood pressure.

In the MIND (Mediterranean-DASH Intervention for Neurodegenerative Delay) diet, food is classified into ten healthy groups and five unhealthy ones. The latter comprises butter and stick margarine, red meat, cheese, fried or fast foods, and sweets.

The recommended consumption from the ten healthy food groups is: six servings a week of leafy vegetables such as spinach or kale, at least one serving a day of another vegetable, plus three servings of whole grains, three servings of beans, two or more servings of berries, and two servings of chicken or turkey each day. A weekly serving of fish is also included, as is a daily glass of wine. All cooking is done with olive oil.

Studies by Morris and others have shown that closely following the MIND diet had a roughly 35% reduction in risk for developing Alzheimer's.

If you enjoy the occasional or regular alcoholic drink, there is good news on this front as well. In a recent study, researchers found that low consumption of alcohol may help to clear the brain. This study at the University of Rochester Medical Center in New York concluded that drinking the equivalent to 2.5 alcoholic drinks per day could reduce brain inflammation.

It was also found to increase the function of the glymphatic system, which is responsible for removing waste products from the brain. High alcohol consumption, however, was found to have the opposite effect, both impairing glymphatic function and increasing brain inflammation.

Lastly, the composition of fat in general in one's diet is believed to play an important role in brain health. Specific recommendations are to consume more vegetable oils and few saturated and trans fats (a fatty acid made through the chemical process of hydrogenation of oils). Doing so is thought to reduce cognitive decline and lower a person's risk of dementia.

Brain-Healthy Foods

Here is a list of reportedly brain-healthy foods, most of which you will also find in many heart-healthy food lists:

> Nuts — eating nuts regularly can benefit brain health by improving attention and memory. In one recent study that examined the effects of eating nuts on brainwave activity the two standout winners were pistachios and peanuts. Other brain healthy nuts include cashews, pecans, hazelnuts, and walnuts.

Nuts have high concentrations of flavonoids, an antioxidant believed to have immense anti-inflammatory, anti-cancerous, and heart protective benefits. Also, flavonoids are thought to lead to neurogenesis, the creation of new neurons as well as improving blood flow to the brain.

Avocados — which are actually a fruit and not a vegetable, are rich in monounsaturated fatty acids known to produce brain cells and help reduce bad cholesterol levels. Also a good source of magnesium and potassium.

Blueberries — contain antioxidants that improve brain health and have anti-inflammatory properties. In a study that looked at the dietary habits of over 16,000 older women across a 15-year period, researchers found that those who weekly consumed one-half cup of blueberries, or at least one cup of strawberries, had slow rates of cognitive disease.

Parents of primary school age children should note that a study has shown that children who eat blueberries before taking exams benefit from a short-term boost to brain functions.

Leafy greens — a study of nearly 1000 adults found that those who ate just one serving per day of leafy greens (spinach, kale, collard greens, and arugula) appeared 11 years younger in terms of their cognitive health compared to those who rarely or never consumed leafy greens. The protective nutrients in leafy greens include vitamin E, folate, lutein, beta-carotene, and vitamin K. Leafy greens are low in carbohydrates and thus a great choice for those preferring a low carb diet.

In a nearly 40-year study that has been ongoing at Washington University in St. Louis since 1979, those who ate leafy greens every day experienced half the cognitive decline as those who avoided these vegetables.

Tomatoes — contain lycopene, a powerful antioxidant.

Fish — DHA, an omega-3 fatty acid found in fish, plays a role in prenatal brain development and improved memory functions in older adults with mild memory complaints. One study showed that consuming omega-3 rich fish just once a week was associated with a 10% per year slower rate of cognitive decline among older adults.

Another study concluded that people who consume fish at least once per week had a 60% lower risk of Alzheimer's disease. Fatty fish such as salmon, tuna, mackerel, herring, trout, and sardines are rich in DHA. It is best to avoid deep-frying fish as the extremely high temperatures kill off some of the omega-3 fatty acids.

Eggs — an excellent and rich source of choline, an important brain nutrient believed to be neuroprotective. Eggs also are rich in B vitamins, which are responsible for fighting the compound homocysteine in the blood. Homocysteine is believed to be a factor in cognitive impairment.

Chocolate — generally the darker the chocolate, the greater are the health benefits. Studies have linked moderate dark chocolate consumption with a lower risk of irregular heartbeats, a reduced likelihood of heart disease, and even a decreased risk for diabetes. More recently, researchers are discovering that eating a small amount of dark chocolate containing at least 70% cacao might have positive effects on both the brain and the body's immune system.

Using electroencephalography technology, researchers found that eating dark chocolate led to a beneficial increase in gamma wave frequency in the cerebral cortical regions of the brain. These are the regions involved in memory and sensory processing.

Additionally, the flavanols in chocolate may improve working memory and visual processing and deter cognitive decline, according to an Italian study. These compounds may also boost blood flow to a part of the hippocampus affected by aging. It is best to avoid "alkalized" chocolate, which has lower amounts of flavanols.

Flaxseeds — rich in essential fatty acids that are not made naturally in the body.

Pumpkin seeds — rich in the mineral zinc, which is important for enhancing memory and thinking skills.

Rosemary — used for hundreds of years as a folk remedy for memory. Even Shakespeare cited its recall prowess, with Ophelia in Hamlet saying, "There's rosemary, that's for remembrance." Now researchers are providing scientific evidence for these ancient claims. In addition to rosemary's

153

ability to reduce stress, act against inflammation, and fight harmful free radicals, it is also a good source of vitamin B, calcium, and iron.

Curcumin — this ingredient found in the popular spice turmeric has anti-inflammatory and antioxidant properties. In India, where turmeric is heavily used to flavor curry dishes, there are significantly lower rates of Alzheimer's disease. Cognitive performance in the elderly is also found to be better in India than in more economically developed societies where overall health care is of a higher standard and more accessible.

Scientists at UCLA have examined the effects of curcumin on people with mild, age-related memory loss. Those who took curcumin over an 18-month period saw improvement in both memory and mood.

Peppermint — a study at Wheeling Jesuit University showed that inhaling peppermint aroma greatly boosts important brain functions, including the ability to reason, solve problems, form concepts, make judgments, and memorize things. Study participants also felt reduced levels of anxiety, increased feelings of calmness, and lower fatigue.

Inhaling peppermint aroma leads to the rise of oxygen levels in the blood, which refreshes and arouses the brain. Other studies have found similar results from drinking mint tea and chewing mint leaves.

Choline — an important brain nutrient that helps to create the brain chemical acetylcholine, which is crucial to normal brain function and cognition. Those who consume high amounts of choline over time appear to have healthier MRI scans of their brains, suggesting that choline intake during midlife may protect against dementia. Good sources of choline are eggs (with yolks), peanuts, fish, poultry, lean beef, broccoli, Brussel sprouts, and dairy.

Lutein — a diet rich in lutein, found in kale, spinach, avocados, and eggs could protect the brain from aging. In a study at the University of Illinois, older people who had higher levels of lutein were more able to match the cognitive pace of younger counterparts than those with lower levels of this nutrient. Lutein displays anti-inflammatory properties and accumulates in neural tissue. Because lutein appears to support both structure and function in the neural membranes, it may be neuroprotective as well. The body does not naturally produce lutein, so it can only be obtained from food sources.

Monounsaturated fats — proven connection to healthy blood flow and lower blood pressure, which in turn helps to keep brains healthy. Found in olive oil, avocados, eggs, and nuts.

Folate — important for memory. Found in walnuts, legumes, asparagus, eggs, leafy greens, beets, avocado, citrus fruits, Brussels sprouts, broccoli, papaya, and bananas.

Vitamin E — diets low in vitamin E have been linked to cognitive decline. As always, it is best to attain vitamins and nutrients directly from food sources instead of via pills and tablet supplements. Good sources of vitamin E are almonds, hazelnuts, sunflower seeds, Brazil nuts, pine nuts, peanuts, Atlantic salmon, avocado, mangoes, Kiwifruit, rainbow trout, and red peppers (capsicums).

Caffeine — a recent study showed that caffeine directly causes a widespread increase in cerebral entropy, the intense complexity and irregular variability in brain activity from one moment to the next. Greater entropy is indicative of more information processing capacity. Using scanning technology on over 60 study participants, researchers discovered that caffeine increased brain entropy across nearly the entire cerebral cortex, and was especially noticeable in the lateral prefrontal cortex, the default mode network, visual cortex, and motor network regions of the brain.

Another recent research study shows that consuming caffeine helps in the formation of memories and in reducing cognitive decline.

Alcohol — moderate alcohol consumption, defined as no more than seven alcoholic beverages per week, provides some brain health protection.

Not all food, of course, is healthy for the brain. Particular foods to avoid, if one wants to focus on eating for brain health, are sugary drinks, refined carbohydrates, foods high in trans fats, highly processed foods, fish high in mercury, and aspartame.

Diet soda drinkers have a smaller hippocampus — the area in the brain that processes learning and memory — according to a study of 4000 subjects. The same study also found that people who drank at least one diet soft drink a day had three times the risk of experiencing strokes and dementia.

In addition, excessive use of alcohol can have serious effects on the brain. Chronic alcohol use results in a reduction in brain volume, plus metabolic changes and disruptions to brain neurotransmitters. Also, people with alcoholism often have a deficiency in vitamin B1. This can lead to a brain disorder called Wernicke's encephalopathy, which in turn can develop into Korsakoff syndrome, a chronic memory disorder resulting from a severe deficiency of thiamine (B1).

Brain Health Supplements

According to the *Nutrition Business Journal*, the sale of supplements touted as memory boosters and brain health remedies practically doubled between 2006 and 2015. And there's been no slowdown since.

However, according to a review of medical studies published in December 2017, there is absolutely no solid evidence that such products can prevent, mitigate, or delay memory lapses, mild cognitive impairment, or dementia. In fact, some may do more harm than good, especially if used with prescription medicines being taken for other ailments. For instance, gingko biloba should never be taken by anyone using blood thinning or blood pressure medicines, or SSRI antidepressants.

The supplements most promoted as memory enhancers are fish oil; B vitamins such as folic acid, B6 and B12; and gingko biloba, an extract made from the dried leaves of a gingko tree.

While studies do show that some people with diets high in omega-3s have a lower risk of dementia, this is only for the

:

omega-3s found in fatty fish such as salmon, mackerel, and tuna. No evidence to date shows the same benefits being derived from fish oil capsules. In fact, a review of thousands of adults who took omega-3 fatty acid supplements showed no fewer diagnoses of dementia or better short-term memory scores than those who took a placebo.

Another study of nearly 3000 adults with memory complaints revealed that those who took gingko biloba extract twice-a-day for five years had no few cases of Alzheimer's disease than those taking a placebo.

The same is true for Vitamin B and folic acid supplements. A 2015 review of several studies concluded that these supplements fail to slow or reduce the risk of cognitive decline in healthy older adults and did not improve brain function in those with cognitive decline or dementia.

The bottom line appears to be it is best to get your nutrients, vitamins, and key minerals through healthy eating practices and not waste money on the unproven claims of dietary supplements. There is no scientific evidence in support of such supplements to boost memory, enhance brain health, or having the ability to slow or reduce brain aging.

Exercise

Too busy to exercise regularly? You may want to re-think your priorities, or your excuses.

Ongoing exercise is known to improve cardiovascular function. According to neuroscientists, exercise also prompts the production of new brain cells, particularly in the prefrontal cortex and hippocampus regions. Research is now showing that as little as 90 minutes per week of physical aerobic activity that elevates your heart rate can protect against cognitive decline. Any aerobic exercise will do — stationary bike cycling, walking, treadmill, or most outdoor activities such as running, rowing, bicycling, tennis, or swimming.

In fact, in a 2017 TEDWomen Talk, Dr. Wendy Suzuki, professor of neuroscience and psychology at New York University stated, "Physical exercise is the most transformative thing you can do for your mind." And, according to clinical sports neuropsychologist Dr. Erin Reynolds, "Exercise is important for the brain for many reasons. Exercise helps regulate hormones and chemicals within the brain that contribute to better moods, improved sleep quality, and overall brain health."

Adds Dr. Reynolds, "Exercise also helps improve cognitive functions like memory and concentration. A regular exercise regimen can help regulate the autonomic nervous system, which may lead to decreased anxiety and an increased ability to deal with life's stressful situations. Exercise is medicine!"

More and more research is proving that getting up from your desk and off the couch throughout the week can have an immense impact on your brain. Some of the ways that exercise changes the brain and improves mental and cognitive health are:

> Improved moods — just five minutes of activity is enough to alter mood states.
>
> Reduces stress and anxiety — exercise helps the body maintain a lower state of arousal at baseline, which results in a reduced likelihood of being easily triggered by anxiety-producing events.
>
> Sleep improvement — people who get 150 minutes of exercise per week sleep significantly better according to a study published in the journal Mental Health and Physical Activity.

Improved cognitive function — exercise plays an integral role in the growth and development of brain neurons.

Protection against dementia — regular exercise lowers the risk of vascular and neurodegenerative disease by improving cerebral blood flow.

Improved focus and concentration — 20 to 30 minutes of moderate to high-intensity physical activity has been shown to have an immediate improvement on focus. Even exercising just once a week improves attention, executive brain function, and planning capabilities.

Memory boost — mild to moderate physical activity, such as walking, yoga, or resistance training helps maintain cognitive health, including improved memory functioning.

In fact, walking and thinking outdoors can lead to a 75% percent uptick in "creative ideation" according to a study in the *Journal of Experimental Psychology*. Additionally, ten minutes of walking up and down stairs can be more effective at giving you energy than half a cup of coffee. This is because pressure waves caused by each stride when walking or running increases the supply of blood to the brain.

Many scientific studies have shown that walking can boost both physical and brain health. According to Stephanie Blozy, an expert in exercise science, "Walking is known to have fantastic physical health benefits, but even a twenty-minute walk can also provide a big boost to your mental health. As you walk, your whole body wakes up — especially your mind."

Harvard Health reported in 2016 that several studies have shown that just 20 to 30 minutes of daily aerobic exercise improves overall cognitive function. Study participants who engaged in aerobic activities, such as walking, performed better on tests and had a quicker and more accurate reaction time.

Walking triggers the brain to release endorphins, the neurochemical that boosts positive feelings in the body and decreases sensitivity to stress and pain. Walking has also been shown to increase Brain-Derived Neurotrophic Factor (BDNF), a protein that is essential for neuronal development, synaptic plasticity, and cognitive function.

How does physical exercise positively help to protect the brain? Firstly, any aerobic exercise program or activity that improves cardiovascular functionality will likely improve blood flow to the brain. And that's a good thing. Secondly, any physical activity causes the brain to release a flood of neurotransmitters. These natural chemicals serve as messengers, enabling cells in the brain and body to communicate and perform optimally.

Three of the neurotransmitters released are the chemicals dopamine, serotonin, and noradrenaline. Combined, these three increase reaction times, improve the ability to focus and concentrate, and improve overall mood. Dr. Suzuki's research also showed that these improvements can last up to two hours after a sweat-producing workout.

Additionally, physical exercise actually changes the brain's physiology, anatomy, and function for the long term. As noted earlier, the prefrontal cortex region of the brain is used for critical thinking, planning, decision making, and control of social behavior. The hippocampus region, a seahorse-shaped region buried deep within the brain, is linked with the formation and retention of long-term memories of facts and events. It tends to decrease in size with age and is one of the earliest parts of the brain to shrink in occurrences of Alzheimer's disease. A larger hippocampus is a sign of good brain health.

:

By increasing the volume and size of these two regions of the brain through exercise, a person has a greater capacity to ward off cognitive decline and to achieve higher rates of cognitive performance. Exercise is also a great stress reducer, thus giving it a double whammy positive impact on your decision-making prowess and competency. And, the more you invest now in improving your body and brain health, the greater is the likelihood of having a high-quality life in your advanced years.

Another study provides additional details on how being physically fit impacts brain health. Researchers at the University of Texas Southwestern Medical Center used imaging technology to study the white matter in brains of participants and compared these with their VO2 max levels during a treadmill exercise. VO2 max is a measurement of how much oxygen is in the lungs during intense exercise.

The study found that participants with higher VO2 max readings, meaning they had better cardiorespiratory fitness, had less deterioration of white matter fibers in their brains. These white-matter fibers are the connection nerves between various parts of the brain, which means deterioration or weakening of these fibers results in the worsening of pathways through which parts of the brain communicate and interact with one another.

In another study, participants who walked 30 minutes four days a week for 12 weeks showed strengthened connectivity in a region of the brain where weakened connections have been linked with memory loss.

Exercise provides immediate as well as long-term benefits. The effects of physical activity, particularly aerobic exercise, on brain health has been well studied and documented. Physical activity induces a cascade of biological processes that improve the functions of the brain regions responsible for memory and decision making.

Research shows that even after just one exercise session people have a greater chance of experiencing positive events and achievement throughout the day and into the next day. After just a few sessions, the benefits of exercise add up. When inactive folks initiated a wellbeing and running program for as little as four weeks, they experienced improvements in memory and reductions in both stress and anxiety.

Another side benefit of aerobic exercise is that it tends to decrease appetite by changing the levels of hormones that drive the feeling of hunger. So instead of being super hungry after an intense workout, the body actually craves less food because exercise reduces the number of hormones that drive hunger from being secreted.

Exercise is not just important for the health of adult brains. It can meaningfully improve cognitive abilities from childhood through old age. In a study conducted by a professor of kinesiology and community health at the University of Illinois, children who regularly exercise displayed substantial improvements in executive function. They were also better at attentional inhibition, which is the ability to block out irrelevant information and concentrate on a given task.

Children who exercised regularly also exhibited heightened abilities to shift between different cognitive tasks. Not surprisingly, those children who attended the most physical exercise sessions during the course of the study displayed the greatest improvements in their respective cognitive scores.

So the proof is in. Exercise is equally as important for brain health as it is for physical health. So what types of exercise are best for the brain? And which other forms of exercise also provide brain health benefits?

163

:

By far and away aerobic exercise is the single best physical activity you can do for long-term brain health. Aerobic exercise is anything that gets the heart pumping faster.

By making the heart beat faster, and for an extended period of time in the 15-30 minute range, blood flow to the brain increases, thus increasing oxygen delivery to brain cells. This is important, for the brain is the biggest user of oxygen in the body.

In May 2018, a review published in the journal *Neurology: Clinical Practice* of almost 100 studies found that older people who exercised for roughly 40 minutes three times a week showed significant cognitive advantages compared with those who did less exercise or none at all. The noticeable cognitive benefits included better information processing speed and superior performance on tests that measured skills like time management and the ability to pay attention.

"This is evidence that you can actually turn back the clock of aging in your brain by adopting a regular exercise regimen," study author Joyce Gomes-Osman, a rehabilitation scientist at the University of Miami's Miller School of Medicine stated.

There is also a growing body of evidence suggesting that the time spent in each single exercise workout matters less than the total time spent exercising over long periods. Hence, it is better to have frequent and shorter workout sessions (i.e. four 25-minute sessions per week) than less frequent and longer ones (i.e. two 60-minute workouts per week).

The latest recommendation from the American Heart Association is to get at least 150 minutes per week of moderate-intensity exercise like walking, or 75 minutes per week of vigorous-intensity exercise like kickboxing, combined with some muscle-strengthening exercises two or more days per week.

Strength training, such as lifting weights and isometric exercises, may also benefit the brain, though the links here are not as clearly established as they are for aerobic exercise. Strength training does increase heart rate a bit, so some blood flow and brain oxygen benefits are presumed. Plus, pumping weights can help grow new neurons and synapses to create more (and better working) gray matter. It may also improve long-term memory.

Most likely, for those who have time and dedication, a combination of aerobic activities and strength training is ideal. In addition to improving brain function, combining these into an integrated and regimented workout routine bestows numerous benefits on the body: muscle strength, cardiorespiratory fitness, weight loss, and reduction in the risks for obesity, diabetes, and hypertension.

Sex

Here is your reward for reading through to the end of this lengthy chapter: a study released in 2017 revealed that having sex while getting older improves brain function.

While few of us would think of sex as exercise, it is nice to learn that it has similar benefits for a healthy brain.

The study by Coventry University and Oxford University in the U.K. involved people between 50 and 83 years old. Those who had sex more often scored higher on tests that measured their verbal fluency and their ability to visually perceive objects and the spaces between them.

The study expanded on a previous research project which had found that older adults who were sexually active scored higher on cognitive tests than those who were not sexually active. At last, neither study demonstrated that sexual activity has any impact on attention or memory, though one day these linkages will probably be proven as well.

Brain Training

While there are hundreds of apps and online programs that proclaim brain training, memory enhancement, and mental agility benefits, there is yet no scientific evidence to support such assertions.

In effect, so-called brain training programs really only make the user better at the particular exercises themselves. Such improvements are not correlated with increases in daily concentration, productivity, or mental acuity. The same applies to non-electronic mental stimulation activities such as crossword and Sudoku puzzles. Solving hundreds of Sudoku puzzles merely makes someone good at Sudoku, but not much else.

As a 2010 scientific study from Cambridge University and the BBC concluded, there is "no evidence to support the widely held belief that regular use of computerized brain trainers improves general cognitive functioning in healthy participants."

In another study, researchers at the University of Southern Denmark randomly assigned about half a group of 95 people (average age early 40s) to a month of mindfulness training using the Headspace app. The other half did Lumosity brain training. Before-and-after measures of performance on a task requiring sustained attention showed that the mindfulness training significantly reduced mind-wandering, while the brain training did not.

The bottom line is that repeating one stimulating activity over and over again does not induce the brain to create new neural connections or to rewire itself. So be leery of new "innovative breakthroughs" in brain training advertised on television and online. While most of these will be stimulating and enjoyable, the only real improvement will be seen in the bank accounts of those promoting these so-called brain tools.

Keep Moving and Learning

Two keys to long-term brain health are to keep moving throughout the day and to stay actively busy well into your post-career years. Sitting too long at a desk, or in conference room meetings, has negative cardiovascular effects, as well as negative consequences for the brain. Researchers at UCLA have discovered that increased periods of sedentary behavior cause a thinning of the medial temporal lobe, a region of the brain important in the formation of new memories.

This study also showed that sitting for large chunks of time during the day is an important predictor of this brain thinning, regardless of general physical activity. This supports the notion that it is good to get up and move about every 45-60 minutes, even if only for a few minutes.

Also, as you get older one of the best ways to maintain brain health and mental sharpness may be to stay busy. In a survey of more than 300 adults over age 50, called the Dallas Lifespan Brain Study, having a busy schedule was associated with better brain processing, improved memory, sharper reasoning, and a better vocabulary. The positive effect of busyness on the brain was consistent across all participant ages, meaning that maintaining a busy and active lifestyle is as important in middle age as it is in old age.

There are, of course, some tried-and-true ways to develop your brain. The first place to start, without a doubt, is with the sleeping, eating, and exercising points above. Others include starting a new hobby, learning new skills, and traveling to new places. Note the word "new" in each of these. The newness of an activity creates an opportunity to learn, which in turn fosters opportunities for the brain to grow and develop. The key is to get out of your comfort zone and away from habitual activities.

Speaking of which, another way to develop your brain is simply to change up your routines. Take a new route to work and notice buildings, parks, neighborhoods, and people. Or routinely change where you walk, noticing different plants, trees, houses, cars, and even mailboxes. These things engage your hippocampus while you are driving or walking, thus stimulating the very home of learning and memory.

In fact, engaging in any activity that is unfamiliar and mentally challenging provides stimuli to your cognitive processes such as attention and working memory. This includes creatively challenging activities such as painting, photography, writing, sculpting, woodworking, and, even cooking. All these stimulate the brain's frontal lobe processing through pattern design, balance, and fine motor coordination.

Learning new skills, such as a new language or how to play a musical instrument, benefits memory, attention span, and brain plasticity. Reading, while less physically active than the options above, helps to increase emotional intelligence, vocabulary, and language skills.

Sadly, according to the Pew Research Center, 24% of American adults report they have not read even part of a book in the past year. This includes no exposure at all to books in print, electronic, or audio formats. Unfortunately, these adults are probably not aware of research from Yale University that found people who read books for 30 minutes a day live an average of 23 months longer than non-readers or magazine only readers.

Reading books creates engagement in the brain that improves many cognitive functions, including vocabulary, thinking and analytical skills, concentration, and focus. This is why one of my favorite hashtags on Twitter is #LeadersAreReaders.

Additionally, reading fiction books impacts empathy, social perceptions, and emotional intelligence.

A frustrating and fun method (as long as you can laugh at yourself) to train your brain is to start using your non-dominant hand for routine activities. To minimize frustration, start with simple tasks like eating or brushing your teeth with the hand not normally used for these activities. Then gradually attempt harder tasks like texting or using a calculator with your "opposite" hand.

If you really want to have some fun with this, buy those workbooks that children use for learning how to write the alphabet and numbers. The ones that have dotted lines that children trace over to form letters and digits. Use these workbooks to teach yourself how to write with your non-dominant hand. It will be slow going at first, but you will be actively stimulating several areas of your brain while making new neuronal connections.

And, of course, socializing with other people in non-work related activities decreases the risk of dementia, increases memory function, and helps to maintain brain health.

CHAPTER 9

Mindfulness

According to the American Mindfulness Research Association, the number of papers on mindfulness published in journals rose from 10 in 2000 to almost 700 in 2016. At the same time, according to PubMed, 42,245 papers were published in 2016 on heart disease alone. So the study of mindfulness is still in its infancy, but is growing rapidly.

Around 4.3 million adults in the U.S. engage in mindfulness meditation, according to a new analysis of the 2012 National Health Interview Survey. Among those exclusively practicing mindfulness, the most common motivations were to improve stress levels, emotional well-being, and general health.

Mindfulness, in its purest form, is simple and easy. You do not need a yoga mat or a sitting cushion. You do not need to learn to chant mantras, repeat phrases, or how to make particular humming sounds. And you do not need to block off significant chunks of your daily calendar to practice mindfulness.

An important point: mindfulness can be practiced within or outside meditation. Meditation is just one of the many methods available for achieving mindfulness. The same goes for yoga.

Also, you do not have to extricate yourself from reality or "go find yourself" in a darkened, quiet space. In fact, rather than trying to escape reality, mindfulness is actually a method for stepping fully into reality and being as close to fully present in the moment as you possibly can.

Mindfulness is not about thinking positively, but rather it is about learning how to think differently and realistically on a more frequent and conscious basis. Mindfulness training and practice also permanently rewire the brain, thus enabling us to change the unhelpful thinking and behavior patterns that can keep us stuck.

In the popular press, mindfulness is often discussed and defined in the context of other concepts, such as yoga, relaxation techniques, meditation, and even therapeutic strategies. And that is because mindfulness can play an important part in each of these. But mindfulness is not limited to a support role and, in fact, is a practice unto itself.

As a reminder, here are the myths and misconceptions we shared with you in chapter one:

1. Mindfulness is more than just learning to meditate. In fact, meditation is not required to become more mindful and present.

2. The purpose of mindfulness is to slow down and observe thoughts without judgment, not to have zero thoughts.

3. Mindfulness is not about taking time out to relax, rest, and tune-out the world. Instead,

mindfulness helps you become more attuned and aware of the world around you.

4. The ultimate goal is not to become mindful all the time, but rather to bring mindfulness into your life on a regular basis to reduce stress, control emotions, improve cognitive thinking, and make better decisions.

Mindfulness is paying attention to the present moment and to yourself in three particular ways: on purpose, in the moment, and without judgment. You can practice mindfulness in a variety of ways, including mindfulness of breathing, eating, bodily sensations (body scans), thoughts, emotions, communication (both listening and speaking), walking, jogging, yoga, tai chi, and many other activities. With continuous practice you can become more mindful throughout the day, not just during dedicated mindfulness practice sessions.

At its core, mindfulness is a self-chosen, self-directed, and self-regulated approach to thinking and awareness that enables a person to disengage (wholly or partly) from the many stresses in life that at times can seem all-consuming. Or, in the words of global spiritual leader Thich Nhat Hanh, "I like to define mindfulness as the energy that helps us be there 100 percent. It is the energy of your true presence."

The simplest way to be mindful is to stop whatever you are doing, mentally or physically, and place your full concentration on the physical sensations of a few deep breaths as they come into and go out of your body. Doing so plants you firmly in the present moment, with a revitalized brain and a greater sense of calmness and control. As author and mindfulness teacher Sylvia Boorstein says, "Mindfulness is awake attention to what is happening inside and outside so we can respond from a place of wisdom."

The most frequently quoted definition of mindfulness comes from Jon Kabat-Zinn, the creator of the Stress Reduction Clinic and the Center for Mindfulness in Medicine, Health Care, and Society at the University of Massachusetts, "Mindfulness means paying attention in a particular way, on purpose, in the present moment, and nonjudgmentally."

In essence, mindfulness is a state of being consciously aware of the present moment and all that it entails. The "particular way" mentioned by Kabat-Zinn in my mind means fully focusing one's attention and awareness on the present moment, while calmly acknowledging and accepting the feelings, thoughts, and bodily sensations that you are having at this particular moment.

In short, mindfulness is a high level of alertness and open awareness that enhances focus, overall attention to the present moment, and the cognitive surfacing of options for solutions and emotional control.

As Kabat-Zinn notes, "The best way to capture moments is to pay attention. This is how we cultivate mindfulness. Mindfulness means being awake. It means knowing what you are doing."

When you focus your attention on the present moment through any mindfulness technique, you immediately become more cognizant and conscious of things in your field of awareness, including sounds, sights, smells, and even the emotional signals being given off by others. But most importantly, a mindfulness pause enables a person to notice what is going on in their own mind and what physical sensations are being felt in various parts of their body.

Being mindful is to deliberately and purposefully pay attention to the present moment, and to fill the mind with one specific point of focus. The immediate benefits of doing so are numerous and integrated:

Full concentration on the task or problem at hand (or of others with whom you are engaging).

A sense of stillness and calm as anything other than the specific point of focus is channeled away.

Increased cognitive processing power as more of the working memory is concentrated on the specific point of focus.

Decreases in emotional outbursts, reactive actions, and regrettable words spoken.

Higher quality decision making resulting from cognitive focus and fewer reactionary decisions or decisions made in fear or under stress.

Reduced levels of stress and the associated health benefits that come with this, including lower blood pressure and decreased risks for heart disease, diabetes, obesity, and Alzheimer's disease.

As you see here, mindfulness is not just about taking a break and focusing on your breathing pattern. That is merely one technique. It is also about being fully present in the moment and leveraging the full power of your brain to deal with the people, problems, or tasks at hand.

Becoming Mindful

Mindfulness is an exercise in focus. The point of the focus can be relaxation, emotional control, interpersonal interaction, cognitive problem solving, or decision making. Astute leaders will use mindfulness in each of these situations, as well as many others.

The brain is wired to think. It is not possible to get the brain to stop thinking, much less to get it to stop thinking about something stressful. The only choice we have is to exert control over the brain through the deliberate practice of focusing attention on one

:

specific thing at a time (mindfulness) to prevent it from being activated by other, stressful factors.

The tricky part is actually deciding to become mindful. We are so used to operating in autopilot mode, rushing from one activity or task to another, that we have no internal mechanism to remind us to occasionally pause and become fully present.

This is where technology can actually help. I have an app on my phone that sends me a simple notification message at random seven times a day. The message reads: *Am I mind full or mindful?* It is the one app that I allow to continue sending me notifications throughout the day. Although I do not receive these messages when I set my phone to airplane mode, at least one is usually waiting for me when I switch out of airplane mode. These messages create seven moments each day to remind me to pause, reflect on what I am doing and thinking, and recalibrate into a mindful state if necessary.

One of the most valuable benefits of becoming mindful, particularly during moments of high stress or difficult decision-making instances, is that mindfulness opens the possibility of choices. An array of choices and options appear in mindful moments because opting to pause prevents habitual, knee-jerk responses from automatically surfacing and taking over. Removing yourself from autopilot mode helps prevent reactive decisions and responses. A mindfulness breather enables your conscious thoughts to hold sway over unconscious and instinctive reactions.

Ongoing mindfulness practice eventually leads to a greater ability to become aware of your own autopilot tendencies and thoughts. This provides you with the option of choosing a different way to respond or act, particularly if any of your habitual tendencies often lead to mistakes, regrets, or interpersonal relationship issues.

If you think that a mindful breathing practice has nothing to do with the workplace, consider the Navy SEALs. Facing some of the most stressful workplace conditions one can imagine, the SEALs use a four-part breathing sequence called Box Breathing. It is a technique that can be done in five minutes:

1. Find a comfortable chair or lie down.

2. Inhale for four seconds.

3. Hold air in your lungs for four seconds.

4. Exhale for four seconds, emptying all the air in your lungs.

5. Hold your lungs empty for four seconds (no inhalation).

6. Repeat for five minutes, or as long as necessary to feel refocused and relaxed.

Personally, I find that taking three to four deep, purposeful breaths using the Box Breathing pattern during any stressful moments provides me with a sense of calm and perspective need to handle any situation more contemplatively and with full focus. Since I use a shortened version of this technique I count between eight and ten at each step.

No longer solely associated with an alternative lifestyle culture, mindfulness and meditation are becoming daily practices used by millions of people around the globe, including corporate executives, celebrities, entrepreneurs, college students, teachers, professional athletes, and just about every other job category imaginable.

Notably, the top download in 2017 in the Apple App Store was Calm, a meditation app. Amazon lists over 1000 books on mindfulness. Corporations are adding mindfulness to their employee wellness programs. Children are being taught mindfulness in school as a way of controlling anger. Mindfulness is going mainstream partly because of science.

Mindfulness has deep roots in the meditation practices of both Hinduism and Buddhism, as well as similar practices in Jewish, Islamic, and Orthodox Christian faiths. However, incorporating mindfulness practices into one's daily life requires no religious belief. Likewise, mindfulness is not counter to any personal religious beliefs or practices.

Mindfulness is a state of complete (or nearly full) awareness. It is gained through the purposeful self-regulation of attention placed and maintained on the present experience, combined with a mindset that is open, curious, inquiring, and accepting. It is a sense of being psychologically and cognitively aware and accepting of the present moment.

This dimension of awareness and alertness is a methodology for clearing and refreshing (some say rebooting) the brain. The main outcome is a slowing, even stopping, of the mind's wandering proclivities. Another important result is halting patterns of fixedness in cognitive and emotional processing.

Some research has suggested that over 60% of a person's thoughts each day can be described as negative or stress inducing (and for some people this figure might be 80% to 90%). Over time, a daily mindfulness practice gradually reduces the number of rambling, discursive thoughts being generated within the mind. If 60% (or more) of these wandering and sprawling thoughts are negative, then perhaps one of the greatest benefits of mindfulness is the reduction or cessation of such mentally and emotionally disturbing roaming thoughts.

One other fundamental principle of mindfulness (in addition to focus and attention regulation, openness to the present and moment) is the nonjudgmental awareness of one's own sensations, emotions, feelings, and thoughts. The key word here is nonjudgmental.

Self-judging of one's feelings, emotions, and thoughts tends to be highly and overly critical. (When was the last time you congratulated yourself for feeling good, joyous, or happy?) Such self-criticism leads to self-inflicted stress, thus hampering the ability to stay within a mindful mode. Being aware of your feelings, emotions, and thoughts without judging these as good or bad enables you to cognitively process these sensations and thoughts without instinctively acting upon them. This, in turn, leads to stress reduction, less fixedness in thought and emotional response, and a greater ability to become calm and relaxed, all of which enhances your decision-making capabilities.

Mindfulness also helps prevent over-reacting to non-emergency situations, such as the daily fire-fighting activities facing most leaders in the workplace. A mindful pause helps delineate a minor brushfire from a three-alarm crisis. Equally as important, a moment of mindfulness helps prevent the kind of reactions that turn minor brushfires into unmitigated disasters threatening performance, results, and interpersonal relationships.

Today's modern thinking on mindfulness was largely sparked by the work of Jon Kabat-Zinn at the University of Massachusetts Medical School. He developed the school's Mindfulness-Based Stress Reduction (MBSR) programs to help patients deal with chronic pain. By getting patients to adopt a mindful approach to pain management, Kabat-Zinn found he could relieve their mental distress and help to improve overall functioning.

His documented successes led to mindfulness being incorporated into a wide range of cognitive and behavioral

:

approaches by other researchers and medical practitioners. This resulted in mindfulness-based treatment approaches for depression, anxiety, addiction, post-traumatic stress disorder (PTSD), Obsessive-Compulsive Disorder (OCD), and even borderline personality disorder. Mindfulness centers and clinics now dot the landscape across the country and worldwide.

More recently, neuroscientists started investigating the links between mindfulness and brain architecture and brain function. This moved the thinking of mindfulness from a therapeutic practice used as a recovery technique for a range of emotional and mental issues to a tool and methodology for improving cognitive performance, reducing the impact of stressful events and situations, and regulating emotional reactions. Today there are mindfulness educational and training programs for business leaders, employees, government officials, prisoners, athletes, medical professionals, combat soldiers, and countless other groups.

Neuroimaging has shown that mindfulness practices modify neural circuits in the brain involved in the regulation of negative emotions. This is one of the many physical changes in the brain detected as a result of mindfulness and mindfulness meditation practices. Studies have also consistently shown that cognitive behavior therapy (CBT), one type of mindfulness practice used by therapists, changes dysfunctions of the nervous system.

According to a survey in the U.K. by the Mental Health Foundation, over 80% of the adult population agrees that the pace of modern life is a major cause of stress, unhappiness, and illness. There is little doubt that each of us could become healthier and more content if we could frequently switch off and slow down.

Being constantly stuck in overdrive is not living. Eventually, the body and brain will tire and break down. Neither are machines designed to operate at elevated levels day after day after day. Mindfulness helps us pause long enough to create some space in our lives — and in our minds — in order to preempt poor thoughts and behavior patterns and to enable better (and different) choices and decisions.

Stanford Graduate School of Business lecturer Leah Weiss teaches a program called Leading with Mindfulness and Compassion. She believes mindfulness in the workplace is important today as "nothing provides more opportunities than the workplace for us to feel discouraged, disappointed, bored, overwhelmed, envious, embarrassed, anxious, irritated, outraged, and afraid to say what we really feel."

In her book, *How We Work: Live Your Purpose, Reclaim Your Sanity, and Embrace the Daily Grind*, she describes three kinds of mindfulness:

> Embodiment — having mindfulness of the body. Being aware of your body as you go through the day, as the body is an important source of information on pain and the physical manifestations of emotions.
>
> Metacognition — the ability to know what we are experiencing as we experience it. It is the ability to observe one's own thoughts, actions, and emotions in the moment. In her words, "By separating the data — what is really happening vs. our interpretation of what is happening — we can find places where we are spinning stories that are not helpful to us, others, or our productivity."
>
> Focus — the ability to direct our attention where we want it. Improving the ability to focus requires retraining the mind to notice in the moment when we are distracted and return to the object of focus.

You may think that having a wandering, roaming mind is not normal. Don't worry, it is absolutely normal. We just do not tell one another about our wandering minds, so many feel that theirs is unusual. Unfortunately, wandering minds are not as happy as focused minds.

While research into the impact of wandering minds is still in its infancy, some studies are already showing causal linkages. A 2010 study reported in the journal *Science* showed that mind wandering leads to negative moods. A more recent study in 2017 revealed that seemingly innocent daydreams and fantasizing about the future can lead to depressive symptoms over time.

There are other significant drawbacks to a wandering mind: reading comprehension, memory recall, and cognitive control over emotions all decrease. Outside of creative activities like brainstorming, innovation, and artistic pursuits like writing and design, where daydreaming can be a powerful tool, focus is the best mental mode of operation for most tasks and decisions. It is definitely starting to be accepted by many in the neuroscientific community that learning to focus the mind has a lot of benefits.

There is an inherent self-regulatory aspect to mindfulness as one takes purposeful control over brain, body, thoughts, and emotions. This comes from the awareness and gathering of disparate and abundant bodily sensations, thoughts, and feelings that evolves into a body-mental-emotional integration and unification. When such an alignment is achieved, a sense of internal self-integrity surfaces.

As Frank J. Ninivaggi wrote in *Psychology Today* (April 2018), this sense of self-integrity "reflects a mind that is clear, openly receptive, balanced, poised, steady, and fluidly mobile without a fixed bottom line (e.g. the need to reach a fixed conclusion) at any moment."

Mindfulness is the self-regulation of:

Attention

Sensory awareness

Perception

The forming of emotions and thoughts

Thinking

Performance

Actions

Your decision-making process

The self-regulation of attention is a difficult challenge for most, but it is essential to the mindfulness process. This is the primary technique for accessing and managing thoughts, feelings, actions, performance, and your internal decision-making process.

Thinking can be exhaustive. Cognitive contemplation is mentally draining. Problem solving, decision making, planning, being creative, negative thoughts, and even daydreaming are all mentally tiring activities. When physical tiredness sets in, accidents and errors start to happen. When mental exhaustion surfaces, bad decisions are made, negative thoughts are voiced, and emotional outbursts spew with volcanic thunder.

The only way to replenish physical energy is through rest and nutrition. The same holds true for mental energy. And the way to rest the mind is through mindfulness or meditation. Mindfulness exercises allow the brain to re-energize and the mind to refresh, refocus, and return to purposeful contemplation.

Mindfulness is a journey, not a destination. It is not something to be added to your daily to-do list, checked off when completed, and then forgotten about until the next day. It is something that is ideally integrated into your daily life and thus practiced (and experienced) throughout each and every day.

Mindfulness works best when it is inculcated into a person's standard operating procedure, something that becomes as automatic as tapping car brakes when a traffic light turns red. Mindfulness is a means of living a fully contented professional and personal life, with increased confidence in one's decisions, thoughts, and actions.

For those of us who are not Buddhist monks meditating in the hills above Dharamshala, cognitive control is the exception, not the rule. At least until we start to implement the tried and proven techniques of mindfulness skills (see chapter 14). But, like any skill, mindfulness proficiency can be learned, practiced, improved, and achieved.

It is just a matter of pausing when elevated stress has us emotionally worked up, taking a few deep breaths, and asking ourselves: *what are the best possible thoughts, emotions, actions, and decisions for this situation here in the present moment?*

Re-Energizing vs. Tuning Out

When you are mentally tired you likely do not have any energy to spare. And it takes energy to listen to one's spouse, deal with teenage angst or disruption, and even to focus on a televised sporting event.

So, how should you cope with life when mentally exhausted?

First, unwind (but don't vegetate). Go for a short walk, knock an easy task off your "honey do" list, or even meditate. Whatever you do, take some time for yourself first and replenish your mental energy stores.

Now you are ready to engage with others. When doing so, continue to focus on your breathing to keep your thoughts from wandering. Pay full attention by listening reflectively. Play back some or all of what the other person is saying in your own words to keep you focused and grounded. Reply with relevant questions, seeking to understand more fully before responding.

The point of mental relaxation is not to get away from it all. The purpose is to prepare and refresh yourself mentally to enable you to get fully back into life. Mindfulness doesn't end at relaxation. It begins there. A bout of mental relaxation provides just enough stability to see what is happening in your mind and to gently inquire about its state.

This is why mindfulness is considered by many as an important practice for mental health. It gives you a chance to perform a quick health check on your mind, just like slowly moving your muscles to check for aches or pausing to contemplate that queasiness in your stomach is part of your daily bodily health routine.

CHAPTER 10

Leadership Mindfulness

The headlines extolling the virtues of mindfulness for leaders have been rampant in the past couple of years. Here are a few samples, all from articles published in 2018:

Mindfulness Isn't Just A Trend, It's Key To Being A Better Leader.

Train Your Brain To Focus. It'll Make You A Better Leader.

Want To Be A More Successful Leader? Try Mindfulness Meditation.

Bring Mindfulness To Your Career.

How Great Leaders Build Trust With 4 Brain-Based Tools.

Mindfulness and Trust: The Keys To Successful Leadership.

Why I Prioritize 1 Hour To Myself Above Everything Else (And Why You Might Want To).

5 Ways To Lead More Mindfully.

Leaders Need To Train Their Minds As Well As Their Bodies.

As the first sample headline states, mindfulness is not just a popular trend. It is a secret sauce to becoming a better leader. How does mindfulness help leaders perform better, think better, and make smarter decisions? In a word: focus.

Leaders have a tendency to spread themselves too thin. They want to have a say in every aspect of every project their teams are working on. They micromanage. They fail to delegate properly. They fear their team members will make a mistake and this will reflect poorly on themselves and their leadership.

And, perhaps worst of all, they want to appear important and busy, to their bosses, to their direct reports, and to their peers and colleagues. Thus there is not a meeting they will not attend nor a conference call invite they will pass up.

Unfortunately, all this busyness pulls leaders — at every level of organizations — in too many directions. And they have little awareness of the present moment, as their brains are still processing information from that last meeting, while simultaneously switching across and trying to prepare for the next one. This level of busyness does not increase productivity. Rather, it raises stress and disconnects leaders from their team members and from being present in any given moment.

Leah Weiss, who teaches at the Stanford Graduate School of Business, links this busyness to the failure of leaders to show compassion and empathy for others in their organization who are also working hard while struggling with frustrations, anxiety over change, and their own stress levels. As she notes, "When we spend so much time with the same people, we sometimes dehumanize them. They become that annoying role or thing that is blocking us."

While conducting research for their book *The Mind of the Leader*, Rasmus Hougaard and Jacqueline Carter conducted interviews with over 1000 leaders. They found that practicing mindfulness helped these leaders engage with their employees, create better connections, and improve company performance.

In a review of mindfulness scholarship published in the *Journal of Management* in 2015, the article's authors noted that research until then had been mostly focused on benefits to the individual practicing mindfulness. This has changed in recent years.

Rohan Gunatillake, author of *Modern Mindfulness: How to Be More Relaxed, Focused, and Kind While Living in a Fast, Digital, Always-On World*, runs Mindfulness Everywhere, the company behind the popular app Buddhify. He says, "Mindfulness, when done well, is really all about other people. Through understanding ourselves, we start to understand other people, because while it might feel like our experience is unique, the reality is that human experience is shared."

His words are important for leaders. This is because recent research has shown that a leader's trait of mindfulness in the workplace is positively associated with various facets of employee wellbeing, including job satisfaction, employee performance, and organizational citizenship behavior.

One study also concluded that individuals high in mindfulness report they are more likely to act ethically and more likely to value upholding ethical standards. Too bad there were no prevalent mindful leadership traits at Volkswagen. Had there been perhaps the Dieselgate emissions cheating scandal would have never occurred.

One important benefit of mindfulness for leaders is that it enhances one's sense of connection to others. Since business results are often a function of gaining alignment with others, the

189

:

ability to connect more succinctly and with greater clarity with direct reports, peers, colleagues, and bosses is an important leadership skill.

Enhanced interpersonal connections also enable leaders to be better communicators and listeners. This helps them to identify areas of unexpressed concerns from team members, as well as to de-escalate workplace dramas and better manage conflict.

The Heart Brain

While we only have one brain, there are neural tissues in both the heart and the intestines. Researchers at the HeartMath Institute call these tissues in the cardio organ the Heart Brain.

While the heart brain does not make decisions, it can have a huge impact and influence on a leader's decision-making process and eventual decisions.

HeartMath researchers have found that the heart has its own complex nervous system that processes and transmits a tremendous amount of information. Perhaps this is why we might say or think, "My heart's not into this task." Or it may explain why we notice when we have only a half-hearted enthusiasm for something. Could the heart brain be telling us something?

Scientists have long known that the brain transmits signals to the heart and that the heart also sends signals (as well as blood) to the brain. But according to the HeartMath researchers, the heart actually sends more signals and information to the brain than it receives in turn. Apparently, our key organs are not just order takers that act when commanded by the brain.

But here is why this discovery is important to leaders. The HeartMath researchers say that "signals from the heart especially affect the brain centers involved in strategic thinking, reaction times, and self-regulation." These are vital functions of effective leadership and apparently are not impacted solely by rational or cognitive criteria.

Using Heart Rate Variability (HRV), scientists at the HeartMath Institute have been able to measure and prove correlations between variable heart rates and physical outcomes. HRV is a measure of neuro cardio function that reflects heart and brain interactions and autonomic (unconscious) nervous system dynamics. Basically, it measures the impact on bodily functions of the heart speeding up, slowing down, or remaining at a steady beat.

When HRV was measured by HeartMath researchers in relation to various physical phenomenon, correlations were found to exist between: 1) health and behavior problems, 2) psychological resiliency and the ability to adapt to stress, and 3) superior performance and tasks related to the brain's executive functions. This linkage is known as physiological coherence, defined as the degree of order, harmony, and stability in the various rhythmic activities within living systems over any given time period.

This research proves that by regulating heart beats a person can improve many aspects of their wellbeing, including cognitive functioning. How does one regulate the beating of the heart? Mindfulness breathing and meditation are two proven methods.

Stress is an obvious reducer and blocker of physiological coherence. As is the typical state of leadership busyness. In these states, the body's defense mechanism overtake the frontal lobes. While this causes variability in heart rate (the heart beats faster when stress is present) it now appears that another vicious cycle is taking place. A faster beating heart is signaling the prefrontal cortex messages of fear, unease, anxiety, and other disruptions. This creates more blockage to the brain's executive control center, causing stress reactions to snowball.

Purposeful breathing and other mindfulness techniques need to be implemented to interrupt this malicious cycle and regain control of thoughts, emotions, and actions.

Mindful Acceptance

The process of observing one's own thoughts — with no judgment or resistance — while accepting the present moment enables leaders to contemplate, ponder, and analyze a difficult situation with calmness and composure. That puts you in a better position to then make mindful choices and decisions immediately or in due time.

Anytime you can control your mind and your emotions from going all over the place, by pausing to purposefully breathe and calmly evaluate a situation, the better will be the options and solutions that arise. A key to this is also accepting the situation as it is, not as you wish it would be or how you hoped it would be.

Mindful acceptance is not about giving up or disengaging from the world. Nor is it a closing of the eyes in the hope a less-than-ideal situation will magically disappear or rectify itself on its own. Rather, mindful acceptance is the ability to observe, acknowledge, and recognize our emotions and thoughts about a situation as these arise in a collected and nonjudgmental manner.

This enables us to go into an in-depth analysis of the problem, its root causes, its links to other problems or solutions, and possible resolutions. This creates greater clarity about the problem and the actions needed to correct or fix the situation. It also leads to higher quality decision making about the remedial actions to be taken.

Mindful acceptance calmly focuses cognitive energy on problem analysis and solution options, rather than on hoping for magical cures or wishing that someone had done something different that could have prevented the current mess. They did not, so do not waste brain energy on that or any "what might have been" thoughts.

Here's a process for implementing mindful acceptance:

1. Bring into awareness a difficult situation you are dealing with.

2. Observe all the negative emotions and thoughts that arise from focused thinking on that situation.

3. Write down these feelings and thoughts and determine the root cause for each (do not worry if several have the same root cause).

4. Write down all the actions you are contemplating, noting which ones may have a negative impact on interpersonal relationships or other situations.

5. Think about your intentions and desire to fix or lessen this difficult situation. Review each one, asking is this the best decision at this moment?

6. Think reflectively on the decisions or actions you are leaning toward. Breathe deeply as you do. Which of these decisions or actions feel internally right? Which one is most congruent with your personal values?

7. Reconnect these decisions or actions with your stated intentions (step 5). Are these in alignment? If so, you are ready to proceed. If not, continue the process from the top at a later time and after some purposeful breathing or meditation as a catalyst.

There is another mindful leadership technique that helps in improving decision making and thinking. It is a Zen Buddhist practice called "the beginner's mind."

By looking at a situation, or a difficult decision, from the perspective of a beginner or novice, you can see things in a new, open, and freed perspective. It is a perspective that is often lost through experience or after becoming exceptionally good at something. In sports, it is called going back to the basics, like how you grip a golf club or how you position your feet before taking a basketball shot.

When we lose the "newbie" perspective we had when we first became leaders, we also lose elements of curiosity, excitement, wonder, and creative problem solving. When you return to seeing things from the perspective of a beginner's mind, you start to once again consciously see all the details and start to ask all the critical questions to ensure the basics are indeed being covered.

The beginner's mind approach is a useful technique to be employed occasionally, particularly when the heart brain is signaling that something critical is being neglected in your problem-solving or decision-making process.

Mindful Focus

The environment for most leaders is one of constant distractions and interruptions. The natural inclination today is to resort to a mode of multitasking. While this may be fine for simple tasks, such as deleting junk email while listening to a conference call, multitasking is the curse of focus and making good decisions.

Using a mindfulness mode increases focus, pushes away any distractions, and enhances productivity and creativity. A mindfulness approach to increased focus entails:

1. Eliminate all potential distractions, including closing the email and Internet message programs on your computer and setting your mobile phone device to airplane mode. Close your door if you have one (and have a Do Not Disturb sign on it if culturally acceptable in your organization).

2. Ensure you have sufficient water, coffee, tea, or other drinks to last at least an hour.

3. Using purposeful breathing to prepare your mind to concentrate.

4. Clear out all thoughts and ruminations, including the mind's chatter about all the other tasks you could be doing (write these down for later reference if necessary to help clear your working memory space).

5. Take two to five minutes to fully focus on the task at hand, remembering to include the most desirable outcome or to picture what success will look like, i.e. "I will finish the first draft of this report before lunch."

6. Get to work. If it is a task that will take several hours to complete, get up and take a short break every 75 minutes or so. Movement creates increased circulation of blood, which is good for the brain. Use this time to replenish liquid supplies, grab a couple of minutes of fresh air, and think of something pleasurable. However, do not access email or engage in conversations that are likely to mentally distract you from returning fully focused to the task at hand. You do not want anything cluttering up your precious working memory space.

195

Becoming a Mindful Leader

Most leaders rely on habitual patterns and tendencies for how they work, usually because these routines have worked successfully for them. Unfortunately, many of these habits and modes of operating are not effective in doing anything but making the leader look busy.

The habits I am referring to are back-to-back meetings, workday calendars overflowing with no scheduled breaks, micromanaging, multitasking, and gobbling down lunch at their desk or workstation while trying to manage email overflow. Leaders simply have a tendency and a predisposition to pack their days and spread themselves too thin.

All this busyness hinders focus, clarity, and quality thinking. Being pulled in too many directions is not conducive to high-quality decision making. Neither is trying to be involved in every decision your teams or direct reports make.

A documented solution for overcoming the consequences of busyness is becoming rooted and fully focused on the present (i.e. mindfulness) throughout the day as much as possible. The good news is that mindfulness is a learnable and trainable skill, and it is easy to get more proficient at this skill through practice and self-awareness.

Here are some techniques for becoming a mindful leader:

1. Be present — notice whenever you are distracted during a conversation, a meeting, or when working alone on a task. Note the distraction, then put it out of your mind. Return your attention fully to the task or conversation at hand.

2. Write it down — if a distraction is a thought about something important, take a moment to

196

write it down for handling later. This frees up working memory that would otherwise be trying to remember the thought or attempting to bring it to your attention. Once you make note of the thought, return fully to the task or conversation at hand.

3. Ask clarifying questions — one of the best ways to stay engaged in a conversation or meeting is to ask clarifying questions. This also helps improve listening skills as you do not want to ask a question unrelated to the discussion or to repeat a question that has already been asked.

4. Stop multitasking — such as responding to emails while listening to conference calls. Doing so is not true productivity, as the chances of missing an important point on the call, or of misreading or wrongly responding to an email, increases when you attempt to multitask.

5. Create time blocks — for important tasks or decision making. Dedicated predetermined blocks of time help leaders focus on one decision or task at a time.

6. End unproductive meetings — is that weekly project status meeting really necessary? Perhaps when the project first started it was. What if it was held fortnightly instead, once the initial ramp-up state has plateaued? As humans, we thrive on momentum. Few things in the workplace kill momentum faster than having to attend a meeting that feels like a waste of time.

7. Break routines — schedule 45-minute or 75-minute meetings, so you can have 15 minutes

between back-to-back meetings to process and encode information from the first meeting before having to prepare and recall information needed for the second meeting.

8. Remember to be compassionate — leaders are leading people, not cogs in an inanimate machine. Compassion is being sympathetically conscious of others' distress with a desire to alleviate it, which should be a stated goal for every leader. Being a mindful leader means observing and understanding how the troops are feeling. It also means being cognizant of how direct reports and team members are likely to react to decisions made and actions taken. A mindful leader never has an attitude of "my way or the highway."

Staying focused and mindfully present is not easy for anyone, especially leaders, in today's world of incessant electronic notifications and constant interruptions by colleagues and team members. Unfortunately, these distractions and interruptions are coming at a cost. And that cost comprises elevated stress, less-than-optimal decision making, unproductive thinking, degraded interpersonal relationships, and less-than-ideal results.

The Perils of Multitasking

A study at Stanford University revealed that regular multitasking makes it difficult for people to focus on a single task. An important finding from this study is that multitasking results in "goal-irrelevant information to compete with goal-relevant information" in the brain. The study results were quite clear, daily multitasking makes a person:

Less effective when multitasking.

Less effective when not multitasking.

Less effective at prioritizing to achieve goals.

When a person multitasks, they literally reduce their intelligence levels, as measured by the ability to comprehend and understand what they are hearing and seeing. A landmark study from York University in the U.K. showed that multitaskers scored 11% lower on a standard comprehension test than those not multitasking.

The evidence is indisputable. Multitasking diminishes mental productivity, elevates brain fatigue, and increases stress. Sandra Bond Chapman, founder and chief director at the Center for BrainHealth at the University of Texas at Dallas and author of *Make Your Brain Smarter*, states frankly that multitasking is "as toxic to the brain as smoking is to the lungs."

The constant electronic notifications from computers, smartphones, and tablet devices are jolting our stress hormones into action. According to endocrinologist and author Robert Lustig, these constant notifications are actually training our brains to be in a nearly continuous state of stress and fear. In such a state, the prefrontal cortex, the part of the brain that deals with the highest-order cognitive functions, is hijacked and basically stops operating.

This results in poor decision making and regretful actions being taken since the prefrontal cortex is no longer in charge. In some ways, this state is similar to the teenage years, before the prefrontal cortex has been fully developed. Not many organizations want their leaders operating with teenage brains!

The keys to preventing this state of multitasking-induced stress and fear are: 1) turning off all but the most necessary notification messages, and 2) stop attempting to multitask.

:

Scientists have known for years what most of us refuse to admit — we really cannot multitask effectively. At least 97.5% of the population cannot, according to research. The other 2.5% have been labeled by scientists as "supertaskers," for they actually can successfully handle more than one task at a time.

So, unless you are definitely one of these elite supertaskers, most likely you can truly focus on only one thing at a time. Hence, every time you pause to check a notification message, or stop thinking about a problem or situation to answer a colleague's question, you pay a price for engaging in that interruption. It is called a "switch cost" and it automatically produces a dose of the stress hormone cortisol.

This, in turn, slows down the functioning of the prefrontal cortex and simultaneously triggers dopamine, the brain's addiction chemical. That, of course, initiates a cruel cycle of unknowingly wanting more interruptions, causing more stress and more cortisol, and then more dopamine. Hence, the desire to continue multitasking so that the desire for dopamine can be fulfilled.

The brain can only process so much information at a time, around 60 bits per second according to scientific research. The more one tries to multitask — which is merely shifting focus from one item to another since the brain can do only one thing at a time — the more this limited information processing power gets distributed across a multitude of tasks or data.

In summary, multitasking, information overload, and constant interruption (from both people and electronic device notifications) are negatively impairing the ways our brains work.

The key to truly developing the sharp focus that leaders need to get the right things done and achieve progress requires working and thinking on a deeper level. Cognitive improvement is only possible when leaders slow down, stop allowing technology and colleagues to constantly interrupt them, and mindfully practice focusing on the task, information, or people with whom they are engaged.

These are the things that mindful leaders do differently:

1. Do not multitask.

2. Cancel electronic notifications and set smartphones to airplane mode for extended periods of the day.

3. Use purposeful breathing as a stress reliever and to drive increased oxygen and blood to their brain.

4. Pause before responding.

5. Focus on the positives.

6. Constantly observe their thoughts and emotions nonjudgmentally.

7. Pay close attention to their breathing patterns.

8. Place importance on self-care, especially in terms of stress control and alleviation.

9. Practice being a good listener.

10. Use mindfulness techniques frequently and regularly throughout the work day.

There are many ways to attain stronger leadership mindfulness. Reducing or stopping multitasking is one of the best places to start. In the next chapter, we will share some of the proven impact that mindfulness has on leaders and the workplace.

CHAPTER 11

The Impact of Mindfulness for Leaders

O ne of the most important scientific discoveries of the current century thus far is proof of the plasticity nature of the brain well into advanced years. While scientists previously thought that brain cells stop growing at a relatively young age, the consensus believed this occurred between the ages of 20 and 30, it is now known that brain cell generation goes on well into the 70s and perhaps beyond.

Equally as significant, scientists are now discovering how meditation and mindfulness can change both the structure and the functions of the brain. These changes can have a direct impact on our behavior and moment-to-moment experiences.

A study released in 2017 by one of the research institutes of the Max Planck Society for the Advancement of Science in Germany linked three common types of mindfulness meditation practices to changes in specific regions of the brain. In the study, participants between ages 20 and 55 engaged in three different types of mindfulness meditation practices, each for three months at a time. The results were nothing short of remarkable.

In the first three-month period, the participants engaged in awareness meditation, whereby they learned to focus their attention and to bring it back when it wandered. Afterward, researchers discovered enhanced thickness in the prefrontal cortex and anterior cingulate cortex areas, both of which are strongly linked to attention.

In the second trimester, the participants employed loving-kindness meditation and worked with partners to enhance feelings of compassion and empathy. After this phase, brain scans revealed increased thickness in the area of the brain known to be involved in empathy.

In the final three-month stage, the participants learned to focus on their own thoughts nonjudgmentally and to augment their understanding of the perspectives of others. Once again, the post-session brain scans showed a direct correlation, with changes measured in the areas of the brain involved in understanding the mental states of others and the perspectives of one's self.

As the authors of the report concluded, these findings "suggest a potential biological basis for how mindfulness and different aspects of social intelligence could be nurtured." They went on to add, "With growing globalization, interconnectedness, and complexity of our societies, 'soft skills' such as empathy, compassion, and taking the perspective of another person, allow for a better understanding of others' feelings and different beliefs and are crucial for successful cooperation."

Learning and incorporating different forms of mindfulness meditation is undoubtedly a very powerful method to boost the "soft skills" that leaders require for future success in today's multicultural, interconnected, and global world of commerce and politics.

In the 1990s, psychologist and author Martin Seligman created the concept of "learned optimism." In several best-selling books on the subject, he showed how we can consciously tamper down our personal negativity bias through learned optimism techniques. In many ways, mindfulness is an extension of Seligman's thinking.

Negativity bias, or the habit of focusing on the risks and downsides of things, is not necessarily a bad thing (when kept in moderation). Such a perspective does help identify potential threats and risks. However, when left unchecked it can freeze the decision-making process or cause less-than-optimal decisions to be made.

Left unchecked for too long, negative thinking and pessimism can become a brain habit that can make you more prone to feeling overwhelmed, burned out, and mentally fatigued. It can also lead you to feel inadequate as a leader, resulting in the much-publicized imposter syndrome.

Ingrained pessimistic thinking automatically turns unknowns into negatives, clouding judgment and making it extremely hard to visualize potential benefits and positive outcomes. Decisions and actions are often paralyzed or postponed, usually in the hopes that new information will arise that will help make a choice clear cut. In the meantime, opportunities are lost and team members frustrated and confused by the lack of decisions and directions from their leaders.

Closely associated with pessimism and negativity bias is fear. Fear is felt when the brain focuses on the uncertainty of future outcomes. It kills opportunities and harms interpersonal relationships, employee morale, and, above all, a leader's self-confidence.

:

Cognitively produced fear requires you to consciously think about the fear-inducing thoughts in order for these to have control over you. This does not apply to emotional fear, which is aroused by a fearful event or unconscious thought.

Now here is the good news about cognitive fear. It can be controlled and alleviated through mindfulness. How? As mentioned in the previous chapter, the brain can focus on only one thing at a time. Hence, when a fear-producing thought occurs, shifting your focus by fully concentrating on another thought or task automatically moves the fearful thought out of your working memory and back into your subconscious. Taking mindful action reduces cognitively produced fear.

Intentionally shifting your thinking and mindset to a more optimistic state through mindfulness activates the areas of the brain involved in creativity and problem solving. An optimistic mindset is also less stressful, thus helping to prevent the prefrontal cortex hijacking described on pages 45 and 84. As such, your decision-making process is less likely to be controlled by fear or irrational emotions, clearing the way for options and data to be cognitively considered through critical analysis.

Learned optimism and mindfulness optimism are both firmly grounded in reality. Neither approach is a carefree, "think positively" methodology based on a pop psychology mandate to have only optimistic thoughts and beliefs. In fact, mindfulness is centered in reality, creating a greater ability to focus on the present moment and to consider all data, sources, and information with more pronounced concentration and cognitive processing power.

Mindfulness Impact on Decision Making

Harried thinking can cause huge mistakes. When you feel out of control, or compelled to make decisions under immense time pressure, chances are the most optimal decisions will not be made.

Yes, business pressures and demands by more senior leaders may result in insufficient time to make an optimal decision. But how hard and firm are these deadline pressures? Most are arbitrarily set by someone, which also means they can be arbitrarily changed if a satisfactory reason is given.

The Principle of Bounded Rationality states that we only have so much time and energy to make rational decisions. When possible, slowing down the decision-making process and ensuring that you are mindfully staying on task during this process leads to better analysis and decisions.

It is not always possible to make fully reasoned and highly analyzed decisions, especially given the pressures and busyness of the typical workplace. But as leaders it is important to ask yourself and others: *can we make an optimal decision without slowing down and being fully focused on the task or decision at hand?* More times than not, the answer is no.

There can be strategic advantages in "slowing down to speed up." Slowing down the decision-making process enables better decisions to be made. It also allows time for greater input and participation in the decision-making process by all relevant team members and stakeholders. This, in turn, leads to greater buy-in for the eventual decision and often means that actual implementation is speeded up and that fewer time-consuming course corrections are required. In the end, well thoughtout decisions lead to better and more fruitful actions and quicker implementation periods.

On the other hand, what if the deadline is firm and unchangeable? This is where mindfulness acceptance comes in

:

and you strive to make the most optimal decision you can within the time constraints given. The questions leaders need to ask in these situations is: *How can we make the most optimal decision within the allotted time? How can we ensure the right people are fully focused on this task or this decision for the duration of the decision-making process?*

Being mindful, meaning being fully present and aware of your own thoughts and feelings, helps leaders better know and understand when they are struggling to make decisions and the real causes behind these struggles. Recognizing your struggles and being aware of your thought patterns, feelings, and emotions are major steps in making positive and meaningful personal change.

Another reason for mindfully moving into an optimistic state when making decisions is that optimism promotes the production of the neurotransmitter dopamine. This chemical not only makes us happy, it also promotes curiosity and a willingness to learn.

A study in Europe mapping the brains of people during puzzle-solving activities found that the moment of inspiration (the so-called aha! moment) when each puzzle was correctly solved was produced by an influx of dopamine into the nucleus accumbens region of the brain. This part of the brain, active throughout the process of problem solving, is part of the dopamine network that is triggered when we receive a reward.

Hence, there is now scientific proof that optimism, by increasing the production of dopamine, can lead to more rewarding puzzle solving and decision making.

Recent research by the INSEAD Business School revealed that increased mindfulness reduces the tendency to allow unrecoverable prior costs, known as sunk-cost bias, to influence current decisions. The study also found that just 15 minutes of mindfulness meditation can lead to more rational thinking when making business decisions.

Participants in the study used mindfulness meditation to reduce focus and thinking on the past and the future, to enable decisions based on information known in the current moment. This type of rational, present-moment thinking was shown to improve and expedite decision making. It resulted in better decisions being made and also prevented decisions from being over-analyzed for weeks.

Taking a mindful pause, whether this is a short meditation session or a clearing-the-head walk in nature, can lead to a more rewarding and effective decision-making process. Clearing the mind is a great remedy for the constant bombardment of information and data sent your way each and every day.

Happier Employees

Studies conducted at the Singapore Management University show that leaders who display mindfulness in the workplace increase employee morale and lead happier employees. This correlation is not surprising since mindfulness is associated with higher quality interpersonal relationships, mostly because mindful leaders are fully present when engaged with others.

Anyone who has observed leaders in action knows that employees are quick to sense disengaged behavior by their managers and leaders. Team members know when leaders are distracted and not fully listening to them. They also know when leaders are distracted or zoning out in meetings.

On the other hand, leaders who are fully present and mindfully engaged with employees make team members feel respected and valued. Such feelings readily translate into higher job satisfaction, increased employee engagement, and greater organizational commitment.

:

The benefits of mindfulness for leaders include:

Less ruminating and obsessing about situations and decisions.

Decreased stress levels.

Reduction in making reactive decisions.

Increased focus on tasks, information, and people.

Close connection to your work, especially important tasks and decisions.

Increased quality of your work and decisions through better use of your cognitive processing capabilities.

Reduced need to correct errors and make course corrections due to interruptions to your decision-making process.

Now, let's take a look at some of the general benefits of mindfulness in the next chapter.

CHAPTER 12

Benefits of Mindfulness

In many ways, mindfulness techniques, particularly mindful meditation practices, help create much-needed headspace. But that is not the only benefit of mindfulness, as this chapter will highlight.

"Over the past ten or 12 years, there has been a vibrant interest in sectors of the neuroscience community in studying the impact of meditation, and now we have the tools," notes Richard Davidson, a psychologist at the University of Wisconsin Madison, in an article in *The Daily Beast*. Also the founder of the university's Center For Healthy Minds, Davidson said, "We can look at brain structure and function and study people repeatedly over time to see how prioritizing mindfulness and meditation impact the brain and change behavior and experience."

Davidson and other neuroscience researchers have begun to discover positive effects to the brain from mindfulness. In a meta-analysis study reported in *Brain and Cognition* in October 2016, researchers found that as few as eight weeks of mindfulness practice can produce long-term structural changes in brain architecture. According to the authors of the report, "Demonstrable functional and structural changes in the prefrontal cortex, cingulate cortex, insula, and hippocampus are similar to changes described in studies on traditional meditation practices."

Meditation has been shown to reduce stress hormones, such as cortisol, while increasing endorphins, dopamine, and other hormones that lower stress and slow the aging process. Meditation also lessens inflammation, which damages and ages cells.

While there are many junk products, apps, videos, and books related to mindfulness on the market, these do not negate the verifiable benefits scientifically proven by respected and stalwart scientists and researchers. Even the National Institute of Health has chimed in, stating that some research suggests practicing mindfulness meditation can reduce blood pressure, symptoms of irritable bowel syndrome, anxiety, depression, insomnia, fibromyalgia, psoriasis, and post-traumatic stress disorder.

Here is more good news about mindfulness meditation, whether you are a leader or not. A 2017 study that analyzed immune system cells discovered that people who regularly meditate had slower epigenetic clocks, a DNA marker of aging. This study used a very small sample size and the results need to be replicated and confirmed in a larger study. But it was the first time that a connection between regular mindfulness meditation and a slowing of the aging process has been seen.

However, what is known through other studies is that cumulative chronic stress speeds up the epigenetic clock. Hence, since mindfulness meditation is a proven stress reducer, the logical hypothesis would be that regular mindfulness meditation is likely to make the epigenetic clock tick at a slower pace.

In fact, mindfulness is proving to be a major weapon against stress. A study published in the journal *Psychiatry Research* reported that anxious people who took a mindfulness course where they learned several different strategies reacted to stress better and had a lower hormonal and inflammatory response to stress than people who did not practice mindfulness.

The folks in the study who learned meditative practices, such as breath awareness, body scan meditations, and gentle yoga, responded feeling less stress than the study's control group. More important, from a scientific viewpoint, these people also had blood measurements of ACTH, a stress hormone released in the brain and then into the bloodstream, that were lower than what was measured in the control group. Additionally, their blood markers of inflammation, called pre-inflammatory cytokines, were lower as well.

"We have objective measures in the blood that they did better in a provoked situation," stated lead research author Dr. Elizabeth Hoge, associate professor of psychology at Georgetown University Medical Center. "It is really strong evidence that mindfulness meditation not only makes them feel better, but helps them be more resilient to stress."

After reviewing dozens of studies analyzing eight different types of meditation and their effects on various heart disease risk factors, the American Heart Association says meditation may help against heart disease. To be clear, the AHA says that meditation can be considered *in addition* to existing standard treatment for heart problems, which include lowering cholesterol, losing weight, and cessation of smoking.

"Our clear message is that meditation may be a reasonable (additional) intervention, but we specifically do not want people to rely on meditation or other such adjunctive interventions in place of proven therapies," notes Dr. Glenn Levine, chair of the AHA and American College of Cardiology task force on clinical practice guidelines.

:

The studies analyzed showed that meditation may help to lower some of the risk factors for heart disease, such as reducing stress and hypertension. As noted above, lowering stress can reduce the levels of stress hormones in the body, which have been linked to a higher rate of heart attacks. Also, keeping blood pressure low can dampen the risk of heart trouble.

One of the research studies analyzed by the American Heart Association was undoubtedly a study released in 2009 that had followed 200 patients for an average of five years. In that study, researchers concluded that high-risk patients who meditated cut their risk of heart attacks, strokes, and deaths from all causes roughly in half compared with a group of similar patients who were given more conventional education about healthy diet and lifestyle.

The meditators in this study also tended to remain disease-free longer and also reduced their systolic blood pressure reading (the upper number, which measures pressure in blood vessels when the heart beats) by five points on average. An earlier study of high-risk patients, many of them overweight or obese, also found that meditation, along with conventional medications, could help reduce blood pressure.

Chronic inflammation is the long-term, runaway activation of the immune system, even in the absence of injury or infection. Such inflammation is at the core of a wide range of health problems, including heart disease, diabetes, cancer, stroke, depression, and Alzheimer's disease. Mindfulness reduces inflammation by impacting changes in the brain's functional connectivity, according to researchers at Carnegie Mellon University.

Brain scans of participants in this study revealed that meditation increased functional connectivity between two brain areas that typically work in opposition — the default mode network, which is involved in mind wandering and internal reflection, and the executive attention network, which is key to planning, attention, and decision making. Additionally, blood samples of the participants who had gone through a three-day mindfulness training program had lower levels of Interleukin-6, a biomarker of inflammation.

The researchers concluded that the changes seen in functional brain connectivity, resulting from the mindfulness training program, appeared to help the brain better manage stress, a known inflammation trigger. Hence, the reduction in stress hormones was directly responsible for the reduced levels of inflammation.

A Brown University study published in the *American Journal of Health Behavior* found a link between a high level of mindfulness and healthy levels of glucose. An unhealthy amount of glucose in the blood is one risk factor for developing diseases like Type 2 diabetes and other aspects of metabolic syndrome. These results are in line with other studies which have shown that mindfulness lowers the risk of obesity and helps people feel a greater sense of self-control over their lives.

In another study at Brown University, people who were not mindful were 34% more likely to be obese. They were also more likely to have increased abdominal fat. Additionally, even those who were not obese as children, but who had become obese as adults, had lower mindfulness scores than people who were not obese in either childhood or adulthood.

Since mindfulness is a skill that can be learned and practiced, those at risk for diabetes and obesity due to lifestyle choices have a skill set available to them to decrease their odds of illness and major health issues should they want. Mindfulness may, in fact, be the best methodology for changing habits that result in a better life.

215

:

Impact on Brain Health

Closely related to everyone's apprehensions about the natural aging process we face as sentient beings are perhaps even heavier concerns and fears related to cognitive decline and associated issues such as dementia and Alzheimer's disease.

Researchers from the University of California Davis Center for Mind and Brain spent seven years following a group of people who regularly meditated. The authors of the study report concluded that meditation can enhance mental abilities and protect against age-related cognitive decline. It is the first study to provide evidence that continued meditation practice over an extended period of time is associated with long-lasting improvements in sustained attention.

The ability to focus, of course, is a trait that often begins to falter with age. A decline in focus ability and attention span is usually a precursor to other negative cognitive effects of aging.

As the researchers wrote in their paper (study results were published in the *Journal of Cognitive Enhancement* in April 2018), "The present study suggests that intensive and continued meditation is associated with enduring improvements in sustained attention, supporting the notion that the cognitive benefits of dedicated mental training may persist over the long term when promoted by a regimen of continued practice."

According to a meta-analysis of all the existing studies on the subject, a simple mindfulness meditation routine can have profound, physical effects on the brain in only eight weeks.

The study, published in the scientific journal *Brain and Cognition* in October 2016, examined 30 studies that used MRI brain scans to measure the physical changes in the brain resulting from meditation practices. Here is the summary of the study results:

> Associated brain changes, in terms of activity levels and volume and connectivity changes, have been reported in the prefrontal cortex (a region associated with conscious decision making and emotional regulation and other functions), the insula (which represents internal body states among other things), the cingulate cortex (decision making), the hippocampus (memory), and the amygdala (emotion).

These results strongly indicate that a mere eight weeks of daily mindfulness meditation is sufficient to rewire the brain to enhance greater focus, increased emotional control, and promote higher quality, more thoughtful decision making.

A group of researchers at UCLA have also been studying the effects of meditation on brain aging. One study they conducted examined how longtime meditators at age 50 compared in cognitive tests with 50-year olds who do not meditate. They discovered a huge difference: those who had regularly meditated for years had brains that were estimated to be around 7.5 years younger than their contemporaries who did not meditate.

The researchers conducting this study concluded that, "These findings seem to suggest that meditation is beneficial for brain preservation, effectively protecting against age-related atrophy with a consistently slower rate of brain aging throughout life."

It does not take much time meditating to generate measurable results. "We've shown in the laboratory that meditating for a half hour a day for two weeks is enough to produce changes in the brain," says Richard Davidson, a psychologist at the University of Wisconsin Madison. "Most people recognize that if you go to the gym for two weeks and work out every day with a personal trainer you'll feel a difference. But those changes aren't going to persist unless you keep exercising. Meditation is very similar. It's

:

a form of mental exercise. And once you begin to experience beneficial changes, it will inspire you to continue practicing for the rest of your life."

"In most parts of the world today, people practice some kind of personal physical hygiene," says Davidson. "My aspiration is that people will care for their minds in the same way. They will engage in simple practices that will be disseminated very widely. I'm convinced the world would be a very different place if we can cross that tipping point."

Impact on Brain Function

According to science, here are five things that happen to the brain during meditation:

1. Cortisol (a stress hormone) levels are lowered.

2. Brainwave activity increases.

3. Dopamine, the so-called feel-good neurotransmitter is released into the brain and body, resulting in a state of deep relaxation.

4. Grey matter in the hippocampus (the region of the brain crucial for learning and memory) increases.

5. Re-wiring within the brain occurs, creating new neural connections.

Meditation increases the cortical thickness in the hippocampus, the part of the brain that runs memory and influences the ability to learn new things. It is also the region of the brain where Alzheimer's disease wrecks so much havoc. So anything that helps strengthen this region of the brain might be beneficial in warding off the onset of Alzheimer's.

Mindfulness has also been shown to help with long-term memory. Researchers have recently discovered a strong connection between memory recall and the conditions under which the memory was originally formed. The study, reported in *Scientific Reports* (May 2018), revealed that calm surroundings contribute to greater memory retention, and that moments of silence actually help to galvanize and strengthen memories. This allows them to be recalled with greater detail, even over time.

Hence, the moments immediately following an event or the intake of new information can impact the quality of the memory that is formed. Thus, having a quiet moment of mindfulness after receiving significant information is likely to do wonders for how well you recall the details of this information later. It is another reason to schedule a few minutes of mindfulness in between your back-to-back meetings.

The amygdala, the section of the brain where fear resides, has less grey matter in meditators compared to those who do not meditate. When the grey matter reduces in the amygdala it correspondingly thickens in the prefrontal cortex area, where awareness and decision making are centered. Long-term meditators are found to be less fearful than non-meditators. They are also seen to have slower reaction times to emotional situations as their larger prefrontal cortexes take the time to respond less reactively.

A study released in May 2017 showed that three months of mindfulness meditation practice leads to a noticeable shift in how the brain allocates attention. The ability to release thoughts that magically pop into the mind is a skill learned through mindful meditation. Apparently, that skill frees the brain to better process rapidly changing things, such as emotional facial expressions and situational events.

:

According to study results at the University of California Davis, gains in the ability to sustain attention developed through intensive meditation training are maintained up to seven years later.

Practicing yoga or mindfulness for just 25 minutes a day can boost the brain's executive functions, according to a study released by the University of Waterloo in Canada. Doing either on a daily basis also improved cognitive abilities linked to goal-directed behavior and the ability to control knee-jerk emotional responses, routine thinking patterns, and habitual actions.

Accumulating evidence from a wide range of studies shows that yoga is good for the brain, as well as the body and overall health of yoga practitioners. Yoga has been used in the treatment of anxiety conditions, depression, insomnia, eating disorders, and other health-related issues. Like mindfulness, yoga helps to reduce chronic stress, which is connected to many physical and mental ailments. Yoga is also known to help reduce the stress hormone cortisol, thus helping to improve mood and emotional regulation.

In addition to helping to keep the body young and in better shape, yoga does wonders for the brain as well. In a 2017 study published in the journal *International Psychogeriatrics*, older adults (defined as 55+) with mild cognitive impairment spent 12 weeks either practicing Kundalini yoga or memory training. As expected, both groups showed memory improvements. However, the yoga group saw a boost in executive functioning and emotional resilience, which the researchers believed was possibly due to the chanting in this yoga method that strengthens visual and verbal skills.

Regular mindfulness meditation appears to make it easier to focus. "Hatha yoga and mindfulness meditation both focus the brain's conscious processing power on a limited number of targets like breathing and posing, and also reduce processing of nonessential information," notes Peter Hall, associate professor at the University of Waterloo. "These two functions might have some positive carryover effect in the near-term following the session, such that people are able to focus more easily on what they choose to attend to in everyday life."

Everyone has more cognitive stress today than ever before and this often prevents or blunts the ability to focus on a given task, problem, situation, or decision. This is particularly true for leaders. Several studies, such as the one from the University of Waterloo, are finding that mental training through mindfulness techniques can reinforce — and even rewire — the neural connections used to drive individual performance and decision making. By taking just ten minutes or so to mentally and mindfully prepare for the next task, while simultaneously giving the brain time to refresh and re-energize, we enhance our abilities to perform at peak levels effectively and efficiently.

In another byproduct finding from the University of Waterloo study, both mindfulness meditation and yoga were effective in improving individual energy levels.

Mindfulness is extremely useful in helping us deal with difficult emotions and the situations or events that tend to trigger strongly felt negative emotions. Mindfulness is used to find a gap between a triggering event or comment and our usual conditioned response. This enables us to use this pause to collect ourselves and change our accustomed response accordingly. In other words, mindfulness helps us learn to make better choices and to reduce habitual reactions that escalate situations or lead to regret.

By taking a mindful moment we get to nonjudgmentally acknowledge what we are feeling and to spot our habitual

:

reactions before they are put into motion. Then we can decide on a different and healthier course of action than usual.

Research by neuroscientist Richard Davidson showed that people who meditate regularly have an enhanced ability to respond empathetically to others without feeling overwhelmed.

Depression and Pain Relief

A review of studies involving nearly 3000 people linked mindfulness meditation with reductions in feelings of depression, anxiety, and even physical pain.

Numerous studies have shown the benefits of mindfulness meditation for patients with depression to be similar to other existing treatments. For instance, a meta-analysis of the effectiveness of mindfulness-based cognitive behavioral therapy at the University of Oxford found that the treatment prevented people from relapsing into depression equally as well as anti-depressant medications. Researchers, however, said it was too early to say that the therapy is better than drugs, but that it "does clearly offer those with a substantial history of depression a new approach to learning skills to stay well in the long term."

Thus far the benefits of meditation appear to be on par with other treatments, but not better. From my own research, I have read of other studies showing preliminary evidence for the role of mindfulness meditation in combating depression that is encouraging, though not yet conclusive. However, at the current rate of scientific inquiry into mindfulness techniques and their benefits, I would not be surprised to learn in the very near future of findings that correlate mindfulness with reduced episodes of depression.

Interestingly, when meditation is combined with regular aerobic exercise, many people reported fewer symptoms of depression. Both meditation and exercise affect the same parts of the brain that have a positive effect on alleviating depression. So it is not surprising that a double-whammy combination of the two works well in conjunction. We just do not have enough scientific proof to substantiate this at the moment.

In a study published in the *Journal of the American Medical Association*, 30% of chronic back pain sufferers reported less pain and improved functionality after receiving treatment that combined mindfulness-based stress reduction (MBSR) with talk therapy. Similarly, in a study of older adults published in the *International Journal of Yoga*, MBSR, combined with sitting or walking meditation, was found to improve quality of life and help relieve pain in chronic low back pain sufferers.

Other Benefits

Incorporating mindfulness into one's life also usually results in a greater awareness and appreciation of the beauty in life. Reducing busyness creates countless opportunities to notice and appreciate the chattering of birds, the colors of trees and flowers, a gentle breeze, and the smells of food cooking.

Raising our mindfulness levels also puts us more in tune with the feelings of others, helps us to notice and share in the joy a child or friend is feeling, and makes us more sensitive to the daily plights others are experiencing.

Getting outdoors and into nature (not the office parking lot!) is profoundly good for us. The proven effects of spending some time with nature include reducing stress, boosting happiness, and aiding creativity. Add one more item to the long list of positive health and wellbeing benefits that can be derived from basking in the glories of nature — attention span.

According to recent research, spending time in a nearby park or any other natural setting may actually double your focus and attention span. Even being able to view nature through windows for 40-60 seconds is enough to refresh the brain and increase attention capabilities.

As counterintuitive as it may seem, short breaks are highly productive in the workplace. One study showed that 20 minutes of yoga could significantly improve brain functioning. Another confirmed that quick naps boost memory. Another study showed that 52 minutes of intense work following by a 17-minute break is the ideal work pattern. All of the studies highlight the importance of recuperation time for the brain in order to achieve peak cognitive performance.

An additional good reason for taking short breaks and moving around a bit throughout the work day comes from another study at UCLA. Adding to previous research showing excessive sitting increases the risks for heart disease, diabetes, and shorter lifespans, this 2018 study used MRI scans to confirm that the medium temporal lobe, which creates new memories, was thinner in people who spent more time sitting. A short break that includes some physical movement will get more blood pumping to the brain, improving cognitive performance when you return to the next task or join the next meeting.

Additionally, for those of you who spend the preponderant portion of the day sitting at a desk or in meetings, the last thing you should do is flop down in front of the television when you get home. Better alternatives include a pit stop at the gym or a short stroll around the neighborhood or in a nearby park.

CHAPTER 13

Shifting Into Mindfulness

There are many ways to shift from busyness and craziness into mindfulness. Each merely takes awareness that you are not fully present in the moment, followed by conscious and purposeful action to pause and become fully present.

The most basic mindfulness method is simply to pause, clear your mind of all but one single thought, and concentrate on your breathing. This can be done with eyes opened or closed, and I find either way works equally well.

Shift your attention to a predetermined thought or find something visual or auditory to focus on. At home, I will close my eyes, shift into a deeper breathing pattern, and listen acutely for the chirps and song notes of birds. In an airport standing or sitting around waiting to board a plane (something I do on a very frequent basis), I will keep my eyes opened, again go into a deep breathing pattern, and focus on observing a worker on the tarmac.

You can even use smell and feelings as points of focus. Take a steaming cup of coffee or tea and hold this tightly in your hands. Segue into a deep breathing pattern and focus on the aroma emanating from your beverage. With each deep breath feel the intensity of the warm cup on your hands and fingers or the powerful aroma filling your nostrils. After a minute or two of this, the peace and focus you feel can be rewarded with a nice long sip of your brew.

If you want to focus solely on your breathing, a good technique is the box breathing technique used by U.S. Navy SEALs to stay calm and aware. Since your workplace stress is unlikely to match that of a SEAL, chances are this breathing pattern technique will work for you as well.

I described this technique earlier (see page 177) and how I use it, so here is a shortened description of this breathing pattern. In box breathing you count in four-second intervals as follows:

> Inhale for four seconds.
>
> Hold breath for four seconds.
>
> Exhale for four seconds.
>
> Hold for four seconds.

Repeat this pattern for eight complete cycles and in just over two minutes you should feel more energized, less stressed, and have greater clarity on whatever is going on around you or within you. Remember, you must focus only on your breathing during box breathing. If a thought enters your mind, simply let it flow in and then out like a receding ocean tide.

Personally, I often extend the box breathing technique to last between five and eight minutes, partially by increasing the interval counts from four to eight seconds. Doing this in my seat while others are still boarding a flight is a great way to remain calm and not get incensed by fellow passengers who violate the carry-on policies.

Another way to quickly shift into mindfulness is to have three or four "go to" words that can bring forth strong visual images in your mind. Each word should represent an image that will help you counter or slow the rise of negative emotions. For me, when I start to feel myself getting angry, my go-to word is sunshine. It is hard (for me anyway) to continue getting angry when I have a picture of bright sunshine and clear blue skies in my mind.

Likewise, I use the word beach to conjure up a peaceful beach scene in the late afternoon when I need to bring forth peace and calmness into a moment that is starting to go elsewhere. If the image is strong enough I can actually feel the cool ocean breeze blowing across my face and body.

Finally, when I am stuck creatively, usually due to distracting thoughts or unwanted interruptions, I use the word waterfall to fill my mind with an image of rushing and bubbling water cascading down a mountainside and into a river below. After a few moments (usually 45 to 75 seconds) internally visualizing this scene I am ready to be fully present in the real moment. Somehow this image of integrated power and unstoppable movement restarts my creative juices and propels me back into full creative concentration (and mindfulness) mode.

Naturally, these three words (sunshine, beach, and waterfall) may not have much relevance to you. Find your own words that can automatically surface meaningful images that will snap you into a mindfulness moment.

For those whose overly active brains have them struggling to get to sleep, transitioning into 5-15 minutes of mindfulness meditation is often the ticket to a good night's rest. Turn off the television and any music with lyrics and simply close your eyes while sitting or reclining horizontally. Once you are comfortable, become perfectly still. Focus only on your breathing (inhaling through the nose and exhaling via the mouth) using the box breathing technique described above. If instrumental music helps soothe and calm you, feel free to have this playing softly in the background. Now head off to sleep.

Purposeful Rhythmic Breathing

We all breathe. Some 23,000 times or so a day. Automatically. Without thinking or consideration. And unless breathing becomes difficult due to a cold, injury, allergy, or a respiratory disease, most of us do not give breathing much thought.

So let's give it a thought. Many thoughts in fact. Concentrated breathing, or what I call purposeful breathing, is also sometimes referred to as breath work. Why? Because it takes concentration and work to focus solely on something that is normally done unconsciously and automatically.

Breathing more deeply and at a slower pace has been proven to have a number of benefits, including relaxing tension in the body, calming nervous shaking, and decreasing blood pressure. Purposeful breathing helps you feel connected to your body, while simultaneously washing away the worries in your head and quieting the mind.

The way we breathe affects the way we think and feel, according to a recent study at Northwestern University. Researchers there discovered that the rhythm of breathing creates electrical activity in the brain, with the effect being slightly different depending on whether a person is inhaling or exhaling.

"One of the major findings of this study is that there is a dramatic difference in brain activity in the amygdala and hippocampus during inhalation compared with exhalation," reports Christina Zelano, assistant professor of neurology at Northwestern University Feinberg School of Medicine. "When you breathe in, we discovered you are stimulating the neurons in the olfactory cortex, amygdala, and hippocampus, all across the

228

limbic system. When you inhale, you are in a sense synchronizing brain oscillations across the limbic network."

This is why breathing deeply calms the brain. It has to do with a cluster of neurons in the brainstem called the pacemaker for breathing. These neurons affect breathing, emotional states, and alertness. Scientists have found that this neural circuit causes us to be anxious when we breathe rapidly and calm when we breathe slowly. Hence, by changing our patterns of breathing we can change our emotional states, as well as how we think and interact with the world.

When we do not breathe well, we do not feel well either physically or mentally. Perhaps knowing this is what led the American Institute of Stress to proclaim, "Abdominal breathing for 20 to 30 minutes each day will reduce anxiety and reduce stress."

Whether you call it purposeful breathing, rhythmic breathing, abdominal breathing, diaphragmatic breathing, or simply deep breathing, a conscious breathing pattern of deep breaths increases the supply of oxygen to the brain and stimulates the parasympathetic nervous system, which promotes a state of calmness.

Breathing deeply means breathing less with your chest and more with your diaphragm. This is easy to determine. Place your right hand over your chest and your left hand over your navel. Take a normal breath. If your right hand is moving, your breathing may be shallow. This can increase fatigue and anxiety. If your left hand is moving, you are breathing deeply and properly.

There are lots of instructions on using the "right" posture to aid breath work. This mostly applies to meditative sessions, not short bursts of purposeful breathing for moving into mindfulness. Personally, I am a big believer in comfort over structure,

:

especially if I am going to be meditating for more than three to five minutes (my daily meditation sessions are 34 minutes).

For a mindfulness meditation session, there are a couple of posture practices I recommend. First, get comfortable either sitting up straight or in a reclined position. A good rule to remember is "health of the body is determined by the health of the spine." As I find it uncomfortable and impossible to sit on futons and floor pillows, I either sit in a lounge chair, on the couch, or lie down on the bed. You will also frequently find me meditating while sitting in an airplane, with a noise-canceling headset covering both ears.

As you begin, relax every part of your body, starting with the toes and calf muscles, working your way up to your jaw and the tiny muscles around your eyes. Be sure to relax your shoulders and tip your chin slightly forward toward your chest to lengthen and stretch your neck. All this body work takes place while inhaling deeply, pausing for a couple of seconds, and then exhaling completely.

Purposeful breathing, which can be done in conjunction with mindfulness meditation or on its own, has a deeply rhythmic pattern to it. The key feature is to inhale and exhale greater than normal, with moments of pause between each inhalation and exhalation.

The process of purposeful breathing begins with a deep, slow inhalation that fills your lungs to capacity. Breathing in through the nostrils is best as this filters the air and is better for oxygen intake. Fill your belly and chest with air as your body starts to expand like an inflatable pool toy. Allow your shoulders and your abdomen to rise and fall with each respiratory cycle. By forcing your abdomen to expand you will also be extending the diaphragm and pushing your ribs out.

As you exhale, push out all the air you can, from both your lungs and your abdomen region. Use a little light force to exhale more deeply than usual. The exhale should be slightly longer than the inhale, as this slows the heart rate. Now pause and notice how your body feels emptied of oxygen. Remain still for a count of four to eight, then repeat the process beginning with another deep inhalation.

Throughout this process focus as much as you can only on your breathing. Without a doubt, other thoughts will creep in, including "this is so boring." Simply cast aside these thoughts and refocus on your breathing. If your mind continues to wander, refocus by silently counting each step in the process: inhale (one, two, three, four, five, six), hold (one, two, three, four, five, six), exhale (one, two, three, four, five, six), and hold (one, two, three, four, five, six). As mentioned previously, the brain cannot process more than one thought at a time. If you are fully focused on counting through each step in the purposeful breathing cycle, your brain cannot interrupt with its own thoughts or agenda.

One point about inhalation through the nostrils. Breathing in slowly through the nose causes nerve fibers in the nasal passages to fire in a slow rhythm, prompting parts of the brain to do so as well. This is why people using slow nasal breathing enter a deeper meditative state than when they breathe at the same rate through their mouths.

One thing I like to do when practicing purposeful breathing during the workday is to go outside (or open a window if stuck inside) and listen for the sounds of birds chirping and singing. Of course, this does not work when I am visiting major metropolitan cities like New York (unless I can get to Central Park) or Tokyo (unless I find my way to the city's famed Shinjuku Gyoen park).

Purposefully listening for bird sounds can even drown out road noise when I am able to fully focus (remember, the brain can only focus on one thing, so in effect it does not hear, or process, the road noise even though it is louder than the chirping and tweeting of the birds). I know the birds do not start singing just because I have stopped to listen. They are chirping away nonstop, whether I pause to hear them or not. Which just goes to prove, what you focus on listening for is what you will hear, if you are mindfully present.

Like any skill, purposeful breathing takes practice and repetition. Do not expect to master this in a week, no matter how simple it sounds. The brain does not appreciate being consciously controlled and it will fight back at first. Eventually, the brain comes to accept and appreciate the calmness and reduced stress that purposeful breathing brings, and eventually consents to this as the new normal.

The purposeful breathing technique can be used any time you need to switch into mindfulness and become more present with yourself, the people around you, and the circumstances and events of the moment.

In The Flow

In 1975, psychologist Mihály Csikszentmihályi first described what he called "flow" and what many of us think as "being in the zone." In this mental state, we are fully concentrated on a task at hand, and hours can fly by like minutes. Some describe this as a "rush" feeling, where all mental (and sometimes physical) energy is dispensed with singular purpose and focus.

Flow is a heightened state of mindfulness. When flow happens, and why it feels so good when it does, is that it results from a perfect match between activity in the brain regions involved in attention and reward. When two brain networks synchronize their activity it smooths the function of thinking, which explains why flow seems so effortless when you are experiencing it. In fact, thinking becomes so automatic and unconscious that you are not even aware of it.

Many athletes describe being "in the zone" as something that happens automatically without their thinking. That is absolutely true, as their conscious thinking is replaced by unconscious thinking in a mindfulness state. Like athletes, anyone experiencing flow is "locked in" and fully present.

Getting "into the zone" or "in flow" is one of the best outcomes of entering a mindfulness state, at least for me. And this is why mindfulness is not an attempt at "getting away from it all," but rather a methodology for "getting fully into it all." As Mihály Csikszentmihályi noted, "The best moments in our lives are not the passive, receptive, relaxing times. The best moments usually occur if a person's body or mind is stretched to its limits in a voluntary effort to accomplish something difficult and worthwhile."

Unfortunately, flow is hard to achieve and difficult to maintain for any length of time. However, the greater your mindfulness levels, the greater are the chances of slipping into flow.

Regular breaks during the workday also create opportunities to slip into mindfulness and flow. Here's advice for leaders from the *Harvard Business Review* (May 2018):

> Schedule 15-minute breaks at least once or twice a day to sit quietly in your office or take a walk. Commit to these breaks as you would any other meeting or appointment; if you don't schedule moments of quiet, something else will fill the time. Solitude gives you the space to reflect on where your time is being spent. Try to get clarity on which meetings you should stop attending, which committees you should step down from, and which invitations you should politely decline.

233

:

As one who takes 10-15 minute "moments of silence" on a regular basis, I can tell you that these are quite happily very addictive. And very productivity enhancing as well.

Moving Into Mindfulness

Here are a dozen ways to move into mindfulness when you are feeling anxious, angry, stressed, or even just overwhelmed:

1. Admit to yourself exactly how you are feeling. Own these feelings nonjudgmentally.

2. Change your thinking from a "worst-case scenario" to an array of other possibilities and potential outcomes.

3. Take a walk, or engage in some other physical activity, to release the anxiety, anger, or other emotions before you act upon these.

4. Use one of your "go to" words to conjure up a visualization that changes your thinking. If you do not have these words and images predetermined, then simply close your eyes and visualize yourself in a calm state.

5. Once your emotions and habitual reactions are in control (through mindful meditation or any of the four preceding actions), think through the situation with a greater focus on rationality. Focus on questions such as, "Will this matter to me a week from now?" and "Am I willing to allow this person, these comments, or this situation ruin my internal peace?"

6. Listen to some soothing music or play a relaxing YouTube video.

7. Go get some fresh air. Being indoors can increase anxiety and anger due to a feeling of confinement. Go outside, even if for only a few minutes. Fresh air will likely help in calming you down, and the change of scenery often interrupts stressed, anxious, or angry thought processes.

8. Change the focus of your vision. Leave the situation. Look away from the other person. Walk out of the room. Go outside. Go grab a coffee or a bite to eat. Just stop staring at the situation or person causing you to be upset.

9. Find a way to relax your body. The body tenses under stress and anger. Sit down and slowly stretch calf, leg, and shoulder muscles. If possible, lie down and slowly relax every part of your body, starting with the toes and working up to your jaw and facial muscles.

10. Write down what is troubling you. Write down how you feel, and how you would like to react if there were no repercussions in doing so. Writing down negative thoughts and feelings helps to get them out of your head. And sometimes crumbling up the paper on which the negative comments have been written and tossing it out has therapeutic benefits as well.

11. Create an action plan for handling the person or situation in a more ideal manner. Maintaining mindfulness focus may help put you in flow, resulting in a higher quality plan of action.

12. Rehydrate or fuel your body with a healthy snack. If you focus on eating or drinking, the

brain cannot continue to ruminate and rerun negative thoughts.

Each of these techniques can be further enhanced by integrating them with purposeful breathing. Additionally, the results will most likely be speeded up when purposeful breathing is used in conjunction with these techniques for easily moving into mindfulness.

In the following section, you will find several purposeful breathing methodologies and exercises that you can practice and use almost anywhere.

Purposeful Breathing Exercises

The 4-7-8 breathing technique was developed by Dr. Andrew Weil. It is a breathing pattern based on an ancient yoga technique call *pranayama*. Some practitioners believe this technique helps them fall asleep in a shorter period of time. Others claim it can soothe a racing heart or calm frazzled nerves.

Prepare for this practice of controlled breathing by resting the tip of the tongue against the roof of the mouth. The tongue needs to remain in place throughout the breathing exercise, which takes some practice as it tends to move down during exhalation. Exhaling during 4-7-8 breathing can be easier for some people if they purse their lips.

Here are the steps for 4-7-8 breathing, completing them counts as one cycle:

1. All the lips to part. Make a whooshing sound, exhaling completely through the mouth.

2. Close the lips and inhale silently through the nose while counting to four.

3. Hold breath for a count of seven.

4. Make another whooshing exhale through the mouth for a count of eight, remembering to keep the tip of the tongue pressed lightly against the roof of the mouth.

Repeat his pattern four more times. The breath holding of seven seconds (or seven counts) is said to be most critical for this breathing exercise.

Another breathing exercise is alternate nostril breathing, called *Nadi Shodhana*. It is a powerful breathing technique that can help relax the mind, calm the nervous system, and clear nasal circulation. Here's how alternative nostril breathing is done:

1. Sit comfortably with the spine straight.

2. Close the eyes and take a few deep inhalations through both nostrils. Exhale through the nostrils.

3. Take the right hand and place the index and middle fingers between the eyebrows as a light anchor.

4. Gently close the right nostril with the right thumb and inhale slowly and deeply only through the left nostril for a count of five.

5. Hold breath for a count of four or five.

6. Release the right nostril and close the left nostril with the right-hand ring finger.

7. Exhale slowly through the right nostril for a count of five.

8. Keeping the left nostril closed, inhale slowly and deeply through the right nostril for a count of five.

237

:

9. Pause after inhalation for a count of four or five. Release the left nostril and close the right nostril with the right thumb.

10. Exhale slowly through the left nostril for a count of five.

11. Inhale slowly and deeply through the left nostril for a count of five.

This alternate nostril breathing exercise should be repeated five to ten times, breathing slowly and deeply as possible. The process may be a bit awkward at first, but you should catch on quickly.

Our minds tend to wander during purposeful breathing exercises. This is particularly true for new practitioners of these techniques. One way to force the mind to concentrate on your breathing process is called square breathing. In this exercise you draw an imaginary square in the air as you work through a purposeful breathing routine, as follows:

1. While inhaling slowly count to four and draw the upward line of an imaginary square in the air.

2. Keeping your focus on the imaginary square, hold breath for a count of four and draw the top line of the square in the air.

3. Exhale slowly to a count of four while drawing the downward line of the imaginary square in the air.

4. Hold empty breath for a count of four while drawing the bottom line to the imaginary square.

Repeat this process up to 10-12 times, either with your eyes opened or closed. Picturing the imaginary square in the air as it is being drawn helps prevent the mind from grasping onto other thoughts.

Another relaxation breathing technique is called Squish and Relax. The squish and relax exercise brings awareness to the body while relaxing tense muscles. For this breathing exercise, lie down with your eyes closed. As you inhale squish and squeeze every muscle in your body as tightly and firmly as you can.

Squish your toes and feet, tighten the muscles in your legs all the way to your hips, suck in your abdomen, squeeze your hands into fists, and raise your shoulders to your head. Hold yourself (and your breath) in this squished up position for a few seconds. Then, while exhaling, fully release your body and relax. Repeat this process three to four more times.

A more strenuous breathing exercise, called the Wim Hof Method, was created by Dutch extreme athlete Wim Hof, an iconoclastic character known for running marathons barefoot across snow and immersing his naked body in freezing temperatures for extended periods. In the course on this breathing exercise is a major warning: "always do the breathing exercise in a safe environment (e.g. sitting on a couch or the floor) and unforced. Never practice it before or during diving, driving, swimming, taking a bath, or any other environments or places where it might be dangerous to faint."

The steps for this breathing exercise are:

1. Get comfortable in a place you won't be disturbed.

2. Do 30-40 power breaths, breathing deeply at a steady pace in and out through the mouth.

3. Inhale fully but do not exhale all the way.

4. After 30-40 power breaths, empty your lungs of air and refrain from breathing for as long as you can.

5. When ready or necessary, take a deep breath in and hold it for 10-15 seconds.

6. Exhale.

The whole process is to be repeated for another three rounds. Wim Hof claims that if you meditate after completing four rounds of this power breathing exercise you should find yourself in a deeply relaxed state of meditation very quickly.

When physical tiredness arises, we are smart enough to take a break and rest in order to prevent exhaustion. But what happens when mental fatigue surfaces? We push on as if being mentally tired is some sort of weakness to overcome. As a result, mental exhaustion occurs.

Mental exhaustion is another cause of poor decision making and poor thinking. The mindfulness techniques in the next chapter will help you prevent mental fatigue and overcome mental exhaustion, thus putting you in a position to make better decisions and create better outcomes for you and your team.

CHAPTER 14

Mindfulness Techniques

L eaders already have tightly packed schedules. So where is the time available to add in some mindfulness practices throughout the workday? Fortunately, you do not necessarily need to free up great quantities of time during the day to practice being mindfully present. This chapter will provide a few ways to add mindfulness to what you are already doing and none of these require more than five to ten minutes to implement.

As always, it starts with breathing. Just breathing a little deeper for a few respiratory cycles at a time reduces any stress signals coursing through your body. Do this repeatedly several times a day and you will notice improvements in your attention span and stress levels. If necessary, use a smartphone app to send you random messages throughout the day to breathe deeply (purposeful breathing).

Awareness of your posture is another way to be mindful. Are you sitting up straight or slouching? Is your neck being strained? Are your leg muscles tight? Noticing the tension in your body can make you realize that you are unconsciously worried about something that you might not have realized was troubling you.

Improving your posture is great, but becoming aware of a hidden concern is even better.

There is a lot being written these days about mindful eating practices. I do not think you need to go all Zen with your lunch each day. On the other hand, taking a few minutes to savor several bites without thinking about email and without glancing through social media or news sites is a good mindful practice, especially if you are eating at your desk. Eating is another of those daily tasks we often handle on autopilot. And like most everything else done in a habitual, unthinking mode, eating provides an opportunity to pause, become centered and present, and switch into mindfulness.

Speaking of lunch, why not have a relaxing lunch break a couple of times a week? Eat outside if possible and comfortable. Incorporate a short 15-minute stroll into the lunch period. Find a quiet place to sit with your thoughts (without judgment) for 10-15 minutes. Whatever you do, be sure to do it without any electronic devices — no checking email, calendars, text messages, or social media. The point is to find a few minutes a couple times a week for some peace and quiet, something that very few of us have enough of.

In addition to breathing purposefully, you can enter mindfulness by walking with purpose. For most, the point of walking, particularly at work, is simply to get from one place to another. Change that by turning walks, even short ones, into opportunities to check-in with yourself: any tension spots in the body? Is your breathing shallow or deep? Are you currently mind full or mindful? What's the single most important thought you should be having at this moment? What has happened in the past 24 hours for which you are grateful?

Focusing on core listening skills is another way for leaders to become more mindful at work. Listening mindfully means giving full attention to not only what is being said, but also to the emotions behind what is being said. Listening in a mindfulness mode helps detect how strongly a person believes what she or he is saying. Being fully present in the conversation also enables a leader to pick up on what is not being said, as well as on any hidden agendas in the room. Additionally, listening mindfully helps prevent leaders from interrupting their colleagues or direct reports, resulting in higher levels of satisfaction, happiness, and employee engagement within team members.

Leaders who practice mindfulness while listening are also more likely to be receptive to original ideas and new information. This openness results in increased innovation and higher quality decision making. Also, such leaders spend less time defending themselves and their ideas, which creates a culture of collaboration and cooperation.

Some people use personal mantras or favorite sayings to push them into mindfulness moments throughout the day. These can be pithy sayings like "happiness begins with me," or motivational messages such as "I am competent, capable, and ready to handle today's challenges."

Others might be simple reminders of deep-seated beliefs. For instance, one of my smartphone apps sends me the message *I am moving forward* at random intervals throughout the day. It also sends me the message *Mind Full or Mindful?* several times a day as well. Seeing these messages reminds me to pause, take a few deep, purposeful breaths, and refocus my thoughts on tasks that are indeed propelling me forward.

Practicing mindfulness at work can help you navigate interpersonal relationships and expectations to achieve optimal results or progress. It also helps you understand and accept that you may not always get the results desired or anticipated. The key is that mindfulness is a foundation for effective work and optimal performance, both for yourself and for your team.

The workplace is rife with harsh and tense conversations that bring forth an array of emotions. Mindfulness can help to allay the temptation to unleash an emotional outburst through a technique called anchoring. Anything you can do to focus on your physical presence and your senses is a form of anchoring. Planting your feet firmly into the floor and observing how that feels is one example. As is pushing your lower back firmly into the lumbar support area of a chair. Some people simply cross their fingers, clasp their hands, or clench their fists (beneath a table or desk, out of sight of others) as a physical reminder to regulate emotional reactions.

Another method for handling tough conversations is to stand up and walk around the room a bit. This activates the thinking part of the brain (prefrontal cortex).

Workplace stress and pressures cause tension to build up in our muscles. Here is a method for releasing and relaxing muscle tension. The key to this technique is to deliberately tense your muscles so that they will completely relax after this exercise.

> Find a comfortable place to sit, preferably in a quiet location. Remove your shoes if possible.

> Start with the muscles in your forehead and scalp. Take a deep breath and then tense all the muscles in this area to a count of four. Relax the muscles as you exhale.

> Continue this tensing and releasing process, coupled with deep breathing, down to other areas in your body that feel tense or sore. Mentally travel throughout your whole body, from the top

244

of your head to the tips of your toes. Pay particular attention to the classic stress accumulation points such as neck, shoulders, jaw, mid back, lower back, and feet.

To be purposeful and creative as a leader you need to create space for yourself.

Here are some ways to incorporate mindfulness practices in the workplace. It is unlikely that you will want to use all of these, so simply pick a few that suit your lifestyle and working conditions. Most of these techniques can be done in five minutes or less, some in conjunction with activities that you are already doing.

1. Take two bites of food or two sips of a hot beverage. Focus on the sensory experiences of taste, smell, texture, temperature, and even the appearance of the food.

2. Take two deep breaths using the 4-7-8 purposeful breathing method (pages 236-237). What sensations stir in your body? How do these breaths make your shoulders, nostrils, and abdomen feel?

3. Remove your shoes and place feet firmly on the floor. Stretch your toes upward as far as you can while inhaling deeply. Feel the stretch of your feet and calf muscles. Relax the toes as you exhale. Now raise your heels as high as you can while taking another deep breath. Note the stretch in your feet and leg muscles. Relax heels as you exhale.

4. Spend a minute observing nature through a window. Which trees are fluttering in the wind?

Any animals about? What image do the shadows make? Which spot looks the most peaceful?

5. Go outside and feel the warmth of the sun and the flow of the air on your skin. How does your body react to this warmth? Can you bring the warmth into your body with a deep breath? Does the feel of the sun on exposed skin make you feel energized?

6. Sit comfortably, close your eyes, and mentally scan your body from toes to head. Where is there discomfort? Pain? Relaxation? Take two deep purposeful breaths while conducting this body scan.

7. Get into a comfortable sitting position, spine straight, and, if possible, shoes off. Spend ten seconds noticing any tension, pain, or pressure points in your body. Then bring both arms straight above your head while inhaling deeply. Be sure to inflate the abdomen first, then your lungs. Hold your breath for three to five seconds while physically tensing every part of your body, from head to toes. Release the tension as you exhale and lower the arms to your side. As you exhale focus your awareness on the tension being released from your body. Repeat this process three to four more times with an unrushed, steady pace.

8. Add two or three things to your gratitude list. What are you grateful for in your life? What good things have happened in the past 12-24 hours? These can be simple things, such as an

unusually clear drive to work this morning, or the way sunlight feels warm on a cool day.

9. Spend a minute reading your gratitude list from the past three to four days. Alternatively, think about something you look forward to doing later in the day or week. Studies have shown that the brain physically changes when gratitude becomes a habit. And a quick reminder of the things you are thankful for will put you in a better frame of mind as you prepare to tackle that next task or go into the next meeting.

10. Stop. Observe. Absorb. Simply stop whatever you are doing or thinking for 60 seconds and pay full attention to what is happening around you. Who appears to be on the edge of anger or frustration? Who is fully focused and concentrated on their work? What is the emotional mood of the room? These are things that leaders need to pay closer attention to, purposefully and mindfully.

11. Stop. Observe. Reflect. Simply stop whatever you are doing or thinking for 60 seconds and pay full attention to your emotions, physicality, and thought patterns. Are you feeling tired? Stressed? Are you on the precipice of anger or frustration? What has been most on your mind for the past hour or two that you have not handled or delegated? What is keeping you from being fully present in the moment? Write these things down and then set them aside (or tackle them immediately).

12. For one minute concentrate only on slowly opening and closing your fists, while breathing deeply. Notice how tension in your hands and arms dissipates each time a fist is opened.

13. Spend one minute mentally recapping the key points from a meeting or conversation that just concluded. What actions were agreed to? What points are still unclear? How are you feeling about the conversation or meeting? What could be done to see improvements the next time this interaction takes place?

14. Send someone mental compassion. Think of someone you want to express compassion for, and then mentally send them some vibes of compassion. Doing so makes you less caught up in your own worries and concerns. Plus it feels good, especially if you follow up later in person with some physical or verbal compassion.

15. To overcome the hazards of sitting too long, give your body a little twist now and then. Start by placing your feet on the floor, approximately in line with the outer points of your shoulders. As you breathe out, slowly and gently rotate your rib cage to one side. It usually helps to bring the hand on the side you are rotating across your body to its opposite shoulder. Your elbow should be pointed down and approximately level with your navel. Hold this position for three to five seconds. As you inhale, bring yourself back to center and elongate your spine by sitting tall. With the next breath out, slowly and gently twist to the other side, hold for three to five seconds,

and then return to center as you inhale. You can easily complete three or four cycles of this exercise with a minute.

This twisting exercise is a healthy internal compression, which gently stretches the muscles near your rib cage while also squeezing your kidneys, spleen, liver, and other organs. As you unwind from these twists, fresh new oxygen, blood, and nutrients are pumping into these organs and the surrounding tissues. It also stretches back muscles that have become stagnant and sore from too much sitting.

16. Stop staring at the computer screen. Look away, at anything else (except a handheld electronic device or mobile phone) for 40 seconds or longer. This helps to reboot the brain and also refreshes the eyes.

17. Slip on your earbuds and listen to a quick guided meditation from a smartphone app. There are hundreds to choose from and most are free, though some do have monthly membership fees attached. A few of my favorites are listed in the Appendix.

18. Find relaxation on the Internet. Sites like rainymood.com and simplynoise.com play soothing noises that encourage the listener to relax and unwind.

19. Eat a raisin with full concentration and focus — what does the raisin look like? How does it feel in your hand? What does it smell like? What does it taste like? How does it feel on the tongue and against your gums? How long does it take

for you to chew it slowly before swallowing? This may seem silly, but I guarantee you it will take your mind off any other thoughts and prepare you to be mindfully present and re-engage.

20. Sniff some essential oils. Studies show that certain scents can have a significant impact on your cortisol levels, your mood, and your productivity. Good scents to use for relaxation or unwinding are lavender, peppermint, and bergamot.

Here are some other ways to gain mindfulness, but these take a little more effort and time than the techniques above:

1. Find some nature. The Japanese practice of *Shinrin-yoku* is known in English as "forest bathing." Research shows that spending some time in nature significantly reduces cortisol and blood pressure while boosting parasympathetic brain activity, the part of the nervous system responsible for rest and equilibrium.

2. Go for a walk for at least 15 minutes, and preferably for a period of 20-30 minutes. This helps to reduce the effects of depression and also gives you the opportunity to focus on other things besides those troubling and stressing you.

3. Color a picture. Adult coloring books are a peaceful way to spend agonizing periods of time (such as sitting on a plane or in a doctor's waiting room) and it is amazing how focused and "locked in" this enjoyable activity can be.

4. Go grocery shopping. Forcing your brain to work through a shopping list turns off mental chatter and negative thoughts.

5. Exercise for 15-30 minutes. Walking, jogging, swimming, weight lifting, stretching, rowing machine, or treadmill. It really does not matter, as long as it forces you to concentrate on the activity with solitary focus.

6. Do yoga for 15-30 minutes. Most yoga practices incorporate elements of both breathing and mindful concentration.

7. Do a crossword or Sudoku puzzle, both of which take enormous concentration and focus.

8. Count backward from 500 using different intervals, such as by four, seven, eight, or nine. At first, this may seem boring, but the harder it becomes the more you will need to concentrate.

9. Listen to music and fully concentrate on the lyrics. What are the meanings behind the words and phrases used?

10. Close your eyes and visualize something pleasant, peaceful, or calm. Within seconds you will undoubtedly feel a slight smile start to unfold. That is a sign that stress and anxiety are starting to be reduced.

11. Prepare a meal from scratch. Even after a stressful day — perhaps even most after a stressful day — washing, chopping, mixing, and tasting ingredients help tune out stress. It also helps to be a little creative, so change the recipe

a bit or try matching different food combinations you have not tried before.

12. Clean your house focusing on one chore at a time — mirrors, floors, vacuuming, dusting, etc. This is not the most fun activity, but you will be rewarded with reduced stress and a cleaner house to enjoy.

13. Brush your teeth while really paying attention to the entire brushing process.

14. Listen to a guided meditation. There are hundreds of apps and websites containing guided meditations of various lengths (a few are listed in the Appendix).

15. Journal your thoughts, including why you are feeling a certain way and what your thoughts are about these feelings.

16. Maintain a gratitude journal by noting five to seven things every day for which you are thankful and grateful. Research has shown that this simple activity is an immediate mood booster.

17. Practice mindful observation by selecting any object and giving it your full attention. How would you describe the texture and the color of the object? How well does it fit in the room, or does it feel out of place? Where do you think it was made? Why?

18. Read a book for at least half an hour, with your phone and all other electronic devices set to airplane mode. Just concentrate on the story and

plot if it is a fiction book, or on the topic and subject matter if it is a nonfiction book.

In the next chapter we will share with you a range of mindfulness meditation techniques that you can implement both in the office and at home.

CHAPTER 15

Mindfulness Meditation Techniques

S cientific studies have shown measurable brain changes resulting from a mindfulness meditation commitment of around 20 minutes a day.

In one study from Canada, researchers proved that 25 minutes of mindfulness meditation generated greater improvement in brain function and energy levels than 25 minutes of quiet reading. The study also showed that mindfulness meditation specifically boosts the brain's executive function and cognitive abilities linked to goal-directed behavior. In addition, the study revealed that mindfulness meditators had a greater ability to control knee-jerk emotional reactions, habitual thinking patterns, and actions.

Getting into a daily routine of mindfulness meditation is extremely easy, particularly with the number of meditation tools, apps, and books on the subject. Frankly, all it really takes is a little knowledge on the subject plus commitment and resolve on your part to set aside 10-15 minutes a day. Once you get started, you are likely to find the experience so enjoyable that you will quickly increase your daily commitment to around a half hour.

One caveat though: mindfulness meditation is not something you simply add to your daily to-do list and then cross it off once your session is completed. Do not treat meditation as another daily task or chore. You must enter meditation with heartfelt desire, so that you can take its benefits along with you throughout the day.

Mindfulness meditation is basically a systematic way to slow down your thoughts enough so that you can effectively watch them. Meditation is not about trying to stop thinking. It is about observing your thoughts from a nonjudgmental perspective.

Learning how to meditate is a continuous cycle of observing your thoughts, getting distracted by a thought, regaining focus, and returning to observing them. Points of focus, such as a phrase or object, are used to slow down the entry of random thoughts and give the meditator something to bring their attention back to when they catch their minds wandering.

Your Non-Stop Brain

You are with yourself all day long, from the time you wake up until the moment you drift off to sleep. Throughout your awaken period your mind is constantly sending you thoughts, wave after wave of thoughts.

It is believed we have roughly 50,000 to 70,000 thoughts a day. Many of them, unfortunately, are not of the useful kind.

If we are not careful and conscious about our thoughts, these unhelpful contemplations and deliberations are likely to impact our decision-making processes, interpersonal relationships, and self-confidence.

How do you catch these unwanted and non-beneficial thoughts in action? How do you prevent them from overriding your emotional controls and paralyzing you from making decisions and taking appropriate actions? The formula is straightforward, though not easy to implement as it likely deviates from your habitual, autopilot thinking practices:

1. Become consciously aware of your thoughts. Stop and observe your thoughts running inside your mind. This is especially important when you are in an emotionally-charged situation, or when facing a major decision.

2. Recognize, identify, and label unhelpful thoughts. Ask yourself: *is this thought serving my best interests and purpose? Is this thought coming from a rational and helpful place, or is it being driven by emotions or ego?* By labeling an unhelpful thought as negative, unconstructive, useless, or obstructive you start to lessen its power on your decision-making process and your emotional response triggers. Let such thoughts go.

3. Select your best thoughts. The ones that are helpful, conclusive, rational, constructive, useful, and enabling. This does not mean only choosing rose-colored, idealistic, and positive thoughts. This is not a "don't worry, be happy" approach. But since you can choose which thoughts to focus on, it makes sense to use the more helpful, supportive, and empowering ones.

4. Bring forth positive self-talk. It never hurts to give yourself a little self-motivation or positive reminders now and then. It may seem unnatural at first to be telling yourself I am capable or I know how to make smart and realistic decisions.

But doing so becomes natural and automatic over time.

The mind is very powerful and it is our choice whether we use this power to make our professional and personal lives better or worse. But we can only consciously make this choice once we start to routinely become aware of our thoughts and then selecting which types of thoughts are going to dominate our thinking, emotional reactions, and decision-making processes.

Meditation

Perhaps the best way to get control over our thoughts is through regular mindfulness meditation practice. Mindfulness meditation can be thought of as working on your mental fitness — an exercise regimen for your brain.

There are three main formats for mindfulness meditation:

Open monitoring — focus is placed on observing the content of thoughts in a nonjudgmental and non-reactive way in order to become reflectively and pensively aware of cognitive and emotional patterns.

Focused attention — placing sustained focus and attention on a particular object, thought, mantra, or image. When the mind wanders, focus and attention is purposefully brought back to the object, thought, mantra, or image.

Self-transcending — uses a mantra, often Sanskrit sounds, which the meditator can attend to without effort or concentration. The goal is for the mantra to become secondary and ultimately disappear as self-awareness increases.

When mindful meditation is practiced regularly (daily is best) and consistently, we create what authors Daniel Goleman and Richard Davidson call "altered traits." They describe these mental states in their book *Altered Traits: Science Reveals How Meditation Changes Your Mind, Body, and Brain* as:

> "lasting changes or transformation of being, and they come classically through having an altered state through meditation, which then has a consequence for how you are day-to-day — and that's different than how you were before you tried the meditation."

Practicing meditation trains your mind to focus awareness on the present and brings a state of calmness and peacefulness into your life. This state is more than just a good feeling, it is also good for your health as well. Meditating benefits your body in many ways, including:

Improving mental health through stress reduction

Boosting mood

Reducing risks for depression

Reducing harmful inflammation throughout the body

Greater control of food cravings, particularly for unhealthy foods and snacks

Preventing or slowing premature aging

Staving off colds

Reducing sensitivity to pain

Likewise, mindfulness meditation has direct benefits for your brain as well:

:

Helping maintain the health of the brain

Slowing natural brain aging

Decreasing mind wandering

Increasing the ability to concentrate and focus

Reducing symptoms of depression and anxiety

Enhancing brain volume and cortical thickness

Aiding in addiction recovery

As in the previous chapter on Mindfulness Techniques, the key to successful mindful meditation is to get comfortable in a quiet place where you are unlikely to be disturbed. Set the timer on your smartphone to the desired length for your meditation session. I started at only eight minutes at first, then I gradually increased this period in two-minute increments every couple of days. Once you are ready, begin to focus your attention on purposeful breathing, trying not to think of anything but the air going into and out of your body.

When you first start to meditate your monkey brain is likely to be full of scattered, often unconnected thoughts. Just let these thoughts enter your mind and then send them away with each breath exhalation.

Meditation Techniques

Most meditation guides will instruct beginners to focus only on their breathing patterns. This is good advice, but often easier to understand than actually follow. I suggest you start out this way, and then within a couple of minutes switch your focus to any one thing that works for you: a single thought, a color, surrounding sounds, or even a mantra or word phrase that has meaning to you. The key objective is to slow down the incoming scattered thoughts until they are all but halted completely.

One good meditation technique for beginners is called the body scan meditation. With eyes closed and purposeful breathing in place, develop a mental scan of how your body feels. Let each part of your body "talk" to your brain by concentrating on these internal body signals.

Start with your feet and toes. Pay full attention to these (and only these) for a few moments. Lightly stretch your feet and toes and notice the sensations this causes. Move upward to your ankles and calf muscles. Again, focus for a few moments then stretch lightly. Continue progressing through your knees, upper legs, hips, pelvic region, abdomen, shoulders, and neck. Then move outward along your arms down to your hands and fingers. Finish with your facial muscles and lips.

Another meditation technique I practice I call the Sunlight Bath Meditation. This is best performed just after sunrise when the warmth of the sun's rays are strong, but not overwhelming or at intense levels of ultraviolet concern.

In this meditation, I sit comfortably in a spot where the sun will directly wash my face for five to seven minutes. With eyes closed, I focus on the warmth of the sun and how its yellow rays bathe my eyelids. Taking several quick, deep breaths I settle in and imagine my body surrounded by this yellow light — a light full of solar energy and power.

I then begin to purposefully breathe in this energy with deep breaths, mentally following the energy into my diaphragm and lungs. With each subsequent deep inhalation, I breathe this energy into other parts of my body (feet, legs, abdomen, arms, etc.). Finally, I take three to four consecutive deep breaths and "breathe" this solar energy into my brain — holding each breath for a count of 12 or longer. This usually results in a "white out" visual sensation of my mind as the solar energy swirls around my brain.

I incorporate the Sunlight Bath Meditation into my longer meditative sessions, especially during autumn and spring when the warm sunlight feels so good in the morning coolness. I find it to be especially invigorating and energizing.

Another mindful meditation technique is a free-form session, where you simply allow thoughts to appear in your mind at free will. Rather than concentrating on any particular thought or sound, in this meditation you patiently permit any and all thoughts and images to pop up uncontrolled.

Focus on becoming aware of the moment when each thought or image appears. As they surface, watch them for a few moments without trying to force them away. Notice how these thoughts rise and fall like waves across your brain. See which thoughts last longest, and which thoughts trigger other thoughts.

The key here is to patiently observe your thoughts and pictures without judgment or emotion. Let them enter and go, rise and fall, uninterrupted and without a response from you. With practice, you will notice how thoughts melt away when you stop reacting, judging, or criticizing them. At first, you may worry about "losing" some thoughts that you want to keep. Don't worry, they are not lost or gone forever. They have just moved on since they did not get a rise or response from you.

Another type of common method for meditating is called a guided meditation. In a guided meditation, an instructor or practitioner takes you through a meditative session. These can be done in person, online, or through a range of smartphone and tablet apps.

Using a calming voice, the guided meditation leader helps you engage in visualization techniques and mental imagery to help you maintain focus during the session. Their comforting voice is often accompanied by soft music or soothing sounds.

Guided meditations are often a good way to get started with meditating, especially since there are hundreds of free guided meditation sessions available on the Internet. One source I particularly like is the website of the UCLA Mindful Awareness Research Center. It has a range of guided meditation sessions in both English and Spanish, each of which runs between three and 19 minutes.

Another good source for free guided meditations is the website of the Chopra Center. These are a bit longer (most are 13 to 28 minutes) and are thus more suited for someone with a bit of meditation experience rather than for those just starting on a mindfulness meditation journey.

Slowing Your Thoughts

For most, the most difficult aspect of mindfulness meditation is learning how to slow down or control your thoughts. Actually, trying to control one's thoughts during meditation is a bit of a misnomer. Slowing them down? Definitely possible. Completely controlling them? A bit on the impossible side, though some regulation is attainable.

The truth is, our thoughts never really stop. However, through mindfulness meditation, we can reduce the intensity, speed, and loudness of our thoughts. And, most important, we can begin to exercise greater control over our actions and decisions by regulating how we respond to our thoughts.

If you try to block your thoughts from creeping into your meditation session, you will undoubtedly end up chastising yourself in frustration. When the mind wanders, allow it to do so momentarily. But rather than focus or concentrate on these thoughts — and then react to them — as is our typical behavior, return your focus to your breathing or your single predetermined meditative thought (color, word, sounds, etc.) and allow any intruding thoughts or emotions to pass through your mind.

263

:

Rather than trying to control which thoughts surface, focus on slowing down the speed at which your thoughts enter your consciousness during meditation. Remember, the brain can concentrate fully on only one thought at a time, so the more you concentrate on your predetermined meditative thought, the less frequent will be the intruding thoughts generated by your wandering mind. The secret to controlling your thoughts during meditation is in not controlling them. Let them enter, slowly. Observe them. Notice them. Then let them slip away or segue into the next thought.

The better you get at not fighting against your thoughts, the sooner you will notice them slipping away. By anchoring yourself in the present moment through focusing on your predetermined meditative thought, combined with purposeful breathing and mental stillness, you will start to become rooted in your true essence. And you will understand your thoughts to be nothing more than mere thoughts, not as truths or facts. The best way to control your thoughts is to observe them without judgment or emotion.

As this happens, you will gain a sense of prevailing peace and tranquility. While this will likely only be for short moments at first, through additional practice and longer meditative sessions these feelings of peace and tranquility will last longer and longer.

By becoming an active observer of your thoughts, you achieve true mental power. You realize you are larger — and more integrated and complex — than your thoughts and emotions. You also realize that your thoughts and emotions need not have power over you. Instead, you can exercise purposeful power over your thoughts and emotions. You can be in control.

Your thoughts, and the speed at which they surface, do not define or determine how "good" you at practicing mindful meditation. This is not a competitive activity, nor is it a zero-sum game. Some days your meditation sessions will fly by with ease. On other days you will struggle to stay mentally focused and still. Accept both experiences non-judgmentally.

Over time, your relationship with your thoughts will change, especially the more you engage in mindfulness meditation. Non-judgment and non-attachment to your thoughts increases with the cumulative time spent meditating. And, with time and practice, your intruding thoughts will rise at a slower pace. Eventually, you may actually reach a point when you become capable of stopping your thoughts completely for extended periods. I am sure you can sense what it would be like to experience the peace and tranquility of such an occurrence.

One other caveat: do not think you can use meditation to withdraw from reality or to escape from the bustle and whirl of daily life. While meditation will give you a respite from the stresses caused by reality and our non-stop world, you cannot turn meditation into a channel of abandonment from reality. Unless, of course, you decide to become a meditative monk and move into a monastery.

Also, be forewarned that mindfulness meditation can become a bit addictive if practiced wrongly. As Jon Kabat-Zinn has noted, "You might be tempted to avoid the messiness of daily living for the tranquility of stillness and peacefulness. This, of course, would be an attachment to stillness, and like any strong attachment, it leads to delusion. It arrests development and short-circuits the cultivation of wisdom."

So go forth and use mindfulness meditation as both a scientifically proven stress releaser and as a conduit for the cultivation of wisdom.

The result will be: Better Decisions. Better Thinking. And Better Outcomes.

:

CHAPTER 16

It's Up To You

There is no excuse for allowing a 60% increase in dementia, Alzheimer's disease, and stroke over the course of the next dozen years.

Please do not become a contributor to this forecast. There is no justification or alibi for becoming a statistic, especially since neuroscience is proving that dementia and Alzheimer's disease are both postponable and maybe even preventable.

You do not want to become a financial and emotional burden for your children. Yet that is the fate that awaits those who do not heed the warnings shared throughout this book.

Better decision making and better thinking — and thus better outcomes — can be yours by focusing on two things:

1) Reducing stress, particularly elevated and extended periods of stress, and

2) Improving the health and functioning of your brain through better eating practices, increased exercise, and mindfulness practices.

The key is to start making better decisions, such as:

Learning to respond, rather than to react, to situations, events, and people.

Pausing to prevent emotional hijacking.

Implementing stress reduction and stress management techniques on an on-going basis.

Increasing daily physical activity now and continuing this throughout your retirement years.

Only you can make the better decisions reduce stress, prevent emotional hijacking, and improve the long-term health of your brain. No one else can do this for you.

It is definitely possible to manage the long-term health of your brain, but you need to start now. This is not something that should be put off until your working days are over. Fortunately, the steps for doing so are straight forward and relatively easy to implement (albeit with determination and persistence):

Reducing stress through the use of mindfulness techniques.

Eating healthier.

Adding aerobic exercise (such as walking) to your daily routine.

Staying active, particularly in retirement years.

Taking proactive steps to go from *mind full* to mindful throughout every day.

Spread the Message

In addition taking care of yourself, you owe it to your family, friends, colleagues, and neighbors to be a conduit for the dissemination of the information and steps in this book.

At work, be a living example of a leader who can transition from a *mind full* state to a mindful one. Use the mindfulness at work practices in chapter 14 to take control of your emotions and increase your cognitive capabilities. Wow your colleagues with better thinking that results in better outcomes. And if you need help, I provide personalized 1:1 coaching on how to go from *mind full* to mindful leadership.

Additionally, bring in our team of expert facilitators and coaches into your organization with our workshops and customized programs. Our workshop *Better Decision Making: Going From Mind Full to Mindful Leadership* is built around the key principles and techniques found in this book.

Together we can make your organization less stressful, more engaging and productive, an even a happier place to work.

Other ways to spread the importance and benefits of becoming a mindful leader in both your professional and personal lives include:

> Join a Mindful Leaders MasterMind Group — where we share monthly updates on brain health discoveries and stress relief techniques. You will also benefit from group accountability partners and our unbiased reviews and recommendations on mindful and brain enhancement technologies.

> Book a Keynote Speech for your organization — my popular keynote talks include *How Stress Impacts Decision Making* and *Why Healthy Brains Make Better Decisions*. Another is *How To Become Brain Healthy and Improve Thinking, Decisions, and Outcomes*. These are ideal for corporate retreats, annual planning meetings, and customer events.

Become a Certified Mind Full to Mindful Leader Trainer — learn how to facilitate our Mind Full to Mindful Leader course content through our train-the-trainer program. This is ideal for independent and in-house trainers and facilitators and includes classroom training, a detailed facilitator's guide, workshop presentation materials, and a license to print participant materials.

I am committed to providing on-going support, materials, and tools for those who truly want to apply the information and techniques in this book within their organizations and communities.

How you go about doing this is up to you. And I wish you great success in doing so.

Recommended Resources

Books on Mindfulness and Meditation

Altered Traits: Science Reveals How Meditation Changes Your Mind, Brain, and Body by Daniel Goleman and Richard J. Davidson

Brain Food: The Surprising Science of Eating for Cognitive Power by Lisa Masconi

Calm Clarity: How to Use Science to Rewire Your Brain for Greater Wisdom by Due Quach

Eat Well, Age Better by Aileen Burford-Mason

Faster Than Normal: Turbocharge Your Focus, Productivity, and Success with the Secrets of the ADHD Brain by Peter Shankman

Flow: The Psychology of Optimal Experience by Mihaly Csikszentmikalyi

Intentional Thiking: Control Your Thoughts and Produce the Results You Desire by Dale East

Make Your Brain Smarter: Increase Your Brain's Creativity, Energy, and Focus by Sandra Bond Chapman

Meditation Is Not What You Think: Mindfulness and Why It Is So Important by Jon Kabat-Zinn

Mindful Manifesto by Ed Halliwell

Mindfulness: How to Calm the Mind and Live Stress Free by Erik Smith

Mindfulness for Beginners: Reclaiming the Present Moment and Your Life by Jon Kabat-Zinn

Mindfulness For Everyday People. Everyday Mindfulness Practice: Simple and Practical Ways for Everyday Mindfulness by Anna Fox

Peace Q: Increasing Your Capacity for Peaceful Living Within and Peace Around You by Jennifer Freed

Super Brain: Unleashing the Explosive Power of Your Mind to Maximize Health, Happiness, and Spiritual Well-Being by Deepak Chopra and Rudolph E. Tanzi

The Better Brain Solution: How to Start Now — At Any Age — To Reverse and Prevent Insulin Resistance of the Brain, Sharpen Cognitive Function, and Avoid Memory Loss by Steven Masley

The Brain Warrior's Way: Ignite Your Energy and Focus, Attack Illness and Aging, Transform Pain Into Purpose by Daniel G. Amen and Tana Amen

The Healthy Brain by Aileen Burford-Mason

The Leading Brain: Power Science-Based Strategies for Achieving Peak Performance by Friederike Fabritius and Hans W. Hagemann

The Mind of the Leader by Rasmus Haugaard and Jacqueline Carter

The Stress-Proof Brain: Mater Your Emotional Response to Stress Using Mindfulness and Neuroplasticity by Melanie Greenberg

The Voices Within: The History and Science of How We Talk To Ourselves by Charles Fernyhough

The Whole Brain Business Book: Unlocking the Power of Whole Brain Thinking in Organizations, Teams, and Individuals. (Second Edition) by Ned Herrmann and Ann Hermann-Nehdi

Train Your Mind, Change Your Brain: How a New Science Reveals Our Extraordinary Potential to Transform Ourselves by Sharon Begley

Why We Sleep: Unlocking the Power of Sleep and Dreams by Matthew Walker

Wired to Create: Unraveling the Mysteries of the Creative Mind by Scott Barry Kaufman and Carolyn Gregoire

Articles

7 Ways Meditation Helps the Brain. PsychCenter, August 19, 2018.

Beyond Meditation – How Leaders Can Put Mindfulness Into Action. Business2Community, September 18, 2018.

Four Ways Meditation Brings Focus to Business Leaders. Forbes, July 9, 2018.

How Thoughts Block Us From Being Fully Present. Psychology Today, August 11, 2018.

How to Control Your Emotions so Your Emotions Don't Control You. Inc. Magazine, August 13, 2018.

How to Start a Mindful Community at Work. Mindful, September 12, 2018.

Mindfulness: Emotional Intelligence Harvard Business Review collection of essays

:

Mindfulness: The Science Behind the Practice. Everyday Einstein, September 4, 2018.

The Real Effects of Unconscious Bias in the Workplace, UNC Kenan-Flager Business School, 2015

What Meditation – And Can't – Do For Your Health. SELF, September 28, 2018.

Why A Daily Habit of Reading Books Should Be Your Priority, According to Science, Inc. Magazine, May 12, 2018.

Why I Meditate and Other Business Leaders Should Too. Forbes, September 4, 2018.

Why We Owe It To Ourselves To Spend Quiet Time Alone Every Day. TED-Ed Blog, June 26, 2018.

Your Brain On Drama: What Social Media Means For Your Personal Growth, Forbes, August 10, 2018.

Meditation Apps

Buddhify

Insight Timer

Meditation Studio

Omvana

Simple Habit

Stop, Breathe & Think

Timeless

Welzen

ZenFriend

Mindfulness Apps

Breathe

Breathe2Relax

Calm

Headspace

I Am

Mindfulness Daily

3 Minute Mindfulness

Websites

BrainChangePro.com

HeartMath.org

MindBodyGreen.com

Mindful.org

PositivePsychologyProgram.com

ACKNOWLEDGEMENTS

There are always numerous contributors and supporters in the background of any published book. I would like to acknowledge and thank a few of these people now.

Karen Coe and Andrew Vujnovich of BrainPro Consulting were instrumental in stirring my interest in recent neuroscientific research and how these findings contribute to peak performance in leaders and individual contributors in the workplace. They continue to be a sounding board for my ideas, while constantly supplying me with new ideas and concepts of their own.

I would also like to thank the many people who took time to read early drafts of this book and provide comments and suggestions, including Alex Chan, Karen Coe, Joe Locetta, Bill McMahan, Bill Molloy, John Petraborg, Nate Regier, Susan Rice, Lynn Schmidt, Bill Treasurer, Wayne Turmel, and Andrew Vujnovich.

Kudos and appreciation go out to Kenneth Ryan Monteclaro whose cover design immediately grabbed my attention and met my creative brief. He was a pleasure to work with as we tweaked his original concept into the final cover artwork.

ABOUT THE AUTHOR

S teven Howard is an award-winning author of 20 leadership, marketing, and management books and the editor of nine professional and personal development books in the *Project You* series.

He specializes in creating and delivering leadership development programs for frontline leaders, mid-level leaders, supervisors, and high-potential leaders. In the past 25 years he has trained over 10,000 leaders in Asia, Australia, Africa, Europe, and North America.

Since 1993 he has delivered leadership development programs in the U.S., Asia, Australia, New Zealand, Fiji, Canada, Africa,

Arabian Gulf, and Europe to numerous organizations, including Citicorp, Covidien, Danaher, DBS Bank, Deutsche Bank, DuPont Lycra, Esso Productions, ExxonMobil, Hewlett Packard, Imerys, Irving Oil, Micron Technology, Motorola Solutions, SapientNitro, Shire Pharmaceuticals, Standard Chartered Bank, and others.

He has been a member of the training faculty at MasterCard University Asia/Pacific, the Citibank Asia-Pacific Banking Institute, and Forum Corporation. He brings a truly international, cross-cultural perspective to his leadership development programs, having lived in the USA for 28 years, in Singapore for 21 years, and in Australia for 12 years.

In addition to his leadership facilitation work, Steven has served on several Boards in both the private and non-profit sectors. He has also chaired a strategic advisory group for a local government entity and a national sporting organization that is a member of the Australian Olympic Committee.

His other books are:

Great Leadership Words of Wisdom

8 Keys to Becoming a Great Leader: With leadership lessons and tips from Gibbs, Yoda & Capt'n Jack Sparrow

Leadership Lessons from the Volkswagen Saga

Asian Words of Success

Indispensable Asian Words of Knowledge

Asian Words of Inspiration

Asian Words of Meaning

The Book of Asian Proverbs

Marketing Words of Wisdom

The Best of the Monday Morning Marketing Memo

Powerful Marketing Memos

Corporate Image Management: A Marketing Discipline

Powerful Marketing Minutes: 50 Ways to Develop Market Leadership

MORE Powerful Marketing Minutes: 50 New Ways to Develop Market Leadership

Asian Words of Wisdom

Asian Words of Knowledge

Essential Asian Words of Wisdom

Pillars of Growth: Strategies for Leading Sustainable Growth (co-author with three others)

Motivation Plus Marketing Equals Money (co-author with four others)

He is well-known and recognized for his truly international and multicultural perspective, having lived in the USA for nearly 30 years, in Singapore for 21 years, and in Australia for 12 years. He currently resides in Southern California.

Contact Details
Email: steven@CalienteLeadership.com

Twitter: @stevenbhoward | @GreatLeadershp

LinkedIn: www.linkedin.com/in/stevenbhoward

:

Facebook: www.facebook.com/CalienteLeadership

Website: www.CalienteLeadership.com

Blog: CalienteLeadership.com/TheArtofGreatLeadershipBlog

MINDFUL LEADERSHIP 1:1 COACHING SERVICE

My objective in individual leadership coaching is to help fine-tune the leadership skills you already possess, and to ingrain new skills, techniques, and leadership behaviors particularly in the areas of regulating emotions, reducing stress, improve brain health, and creating better habits that lead better decisions, better thinking, and better outcomes.

Coaching sessions are 60 or 90 minutes in length and typically focus on two or more of the following topics in each session:

Stress management and stress relief techniques

Brain health tactics

Mindfulness techniques and practice

Meditation techniques and practice

Knowing your stress and emotional triggers

Listening to your body signals

Observing your thoughts

Mindful leadership coaching is conducted both face-to-face and via video calls. To discuss your needs give me a call at (760) 835-7870.

Join Our Exclusive
Mindful Leaders
MasterMind Groups

Join fellow mindful leaders monthly to exchange information, tips, and news on brain health discoveries, stress relief techniques, and other mindful leadership best practices.

Benefit from group accountability partners and receive unbiased reviews and recommendations on mindfulness and healthy brain technologies. Regular guest speakers are another highlight enjoyed by Mindful Leaders MasterMind Group members.

Each Mindful Leaders MasterMind Group is limited to 15 participants and will meet monthly on conference and video calls. All sessions will be led by a member of our Mindful Leaders MasterMind Board.

For details on how to join, contact me via email at: Steven@CalienteLeadership.com.

KEYNOTE SPEAKING

An accomplished platform speaker, Steven Howard is available as a Keynote Speaker for public and corporate conferences, off-site meetings, sales conferences, and association meetings.

His Mindful Leadership keynote topics include:

How Stress Impacts Your Decision Making

Why Healthy Brains Make Better Decisions

Better Decisions. Better Thinking. Better Outcomes. Going from *Mind Full* to Mindful Leadership

How to Become Brain Healthy and Improve Decisions, Thinking, and Outcomes.

A dynamic, enthusiastic and entertaining speaker, Steven is known for challenging audiences to think in new directors and to make connections they have never made before.

For booking availability, contact steven@CalienteLeadership.com.

CORPORATE WORKSHOPS

Decision-making is a fundamental component of every leader's daily life, both professionally and personally. Unfortunately, stress and other factors often lead good leaders to make bad decisions.

The daily juggling of data, reports, email, meetings, decisions, and way too much information makes it difficult to cope and results in leaders running on autopilot. We see these zoned out and inattentive leaders struggling to lead their teams and team members, as well as themselves.

Many leaders are so consumed with firefighting activities that few realize these fires have been caused by the bad decisions and choices they have made. Thus the cycle of stress-induced poor decision making is perpetuated by the stress of correcting unanticipated results from previous poor decisions.

No wonder so many leaders operate in a "mind full" mode. This is not good. A more effective method is to make decisions in a "mindful" mode. Fortunately, this is a skill that can be learned, ingrained, and practiced.

That's why we created our one-day workshop *Better Decision Making: Shifting From Mind Full to Mindful Leadership Skills*. In this workshop leaders and managers will learn:

How stress leads to bad decision making.

How mindfulness can impact thoughts, reactions, and behaviors.

How to use mindfulness to make better decisions.

How to use mindfulness to reduce unconscious bias in decision making.

How to easily shift into mindfulness with practical techniques and tips.

The benefits of mindfulness on attention, memory, people skills, and personal health.

A range of methods for improving brain health.

Why practicing mindfulness produces better results than so-called brain training activities.

Contact us today (steven@calienteleadership.com or 760-835-7870) to discuss how to benefit from *Better Decision Making: Shifting from Mind Full to Mindful Leadership Skills* for yourself, your team, or your entire organization.

BECOME A MIND FULL TO MINDFUL LEADERSHIP CERTIFIED TRAINER

Want to add new content to your training portfolio? We are certifying trainers and facilitators to deliver our *Better Decision Making: Shifting from Mind Full to Mindful Leadership Skills* full-day workshop to your own clients and customers.

Certified trainers will receive complete workshop materials, a detailed facilitator's guide, and a license to print participant materials. You will also have access to a monthly MasterMind session, free content updates, and a license to conduct both public events and corporate workshops. You can also earn sales commissions on keynote speaking and coaching services you send to us.

Certification takes place over a 2.5-day Train-the-Trainer program. These programs are currently scheduled in 2019 for:

Palm Springs, CA	Jan 16-18
Orlando, FL	Feb 27 – Mar 1
Dallas, TX	May 16-18
Washington, DC	May 22-24

In-house TTT programs for organizations can be scheduled at your location and convenience. For more details, please see: www.CalienteLeadership.com/Facilitation-Certification.

:

11371930R00166

Made in the USA
San Bernardino, CA
04 December 2018